The Adornment of the Spiritual Marriage

)

The Adornment

of the

Spiritual Marriage

The Sparkling Stone
&
The Book of Supreme Truth

Translated from

the Flemish

by

C. A. Wynschenk Dom

Introduction

by

Allan Armstrong

Ibis Press
An Imprint of Nicolas-Hays, Inc.
Berwick, Maine

Published in 2005 by
Ibis Press, an imprint of Nicolas-Hays, Inc., P. O. Box 1126,
Berwick, ME 03901-1126; www.nicolashays.com
Distributed to the trade by Red Wheel/Weiser, LLC, P. O. Box 612,
York Beach, ME 03910-0612; www.redwheelweiser.com

Library of Congress Cataloging-in-Publication Data
Ruusbroec, Jan van, 1293-1381.
    [Selections. English. 2005]
    The adornment of the spiritual marriage ; with, The book of
supreme truth ; &, The sparkling stone / Jan van Ruysbroeck ;
introduction by Allan Armstrong ; translator, C.A. Wynschenk.--
Adornment of the spiritual marriage ; with, The book of supreme
truth ; &, The sparkling stone
    p. cm. -- (The Ibis western mystery tradition series)
    Originally published: The adornment of the spiritual marriage ;
The sparkling stone ; The book of supreme truth. London : J.M.
Dent ; New York : E.P. Dutton, 1916. With new introd.
    Includes bibliographical references.
    ISBN 0-89254-140-7 (trade pbk.)
    1. Mysticism--Catholic Church--Early works to 1800. 2. Catholic
Church--Doctrines--Early works to 1800. I. Wynschenk, C. A. II.
Title. III. Series.
    BV5080.R88213 2005 248.2'2--dc22   2004056752

VG
Printed in the United States of America
11   10   09   08   07   06   05
7   6   5   4   3   2   1

Cover design by Kathryn Sky-Peck.

CONTENTS

Contents

Contents

THE SPARKLING STONE

THE BOOK OF SUPREME TRUTH

INTRODUCTION

THE BLESSED JOHN RUYSBROECK

In the year 1304 or thereabouts, without leave or warning, an eleven-year-old Flemish boy left the comfort and security of home in the little country village of Ruysbroeck, and made his way through the great forest of Soignes to the city of Brussels to place himself under the tutelage of his uncle, the Reverend Jan Hinckaert, a priest and canon of the Cathedral of St. Gudule. It is tempting to imagine this young boy, bag in hand, containing a few modest possessions and some provisions for his journey, slipping quietly out of the door of his family home into the early hours of the morning, perhaps as light was just breaking, and setting out in all innocence, inspired and guided by the Holy Spirit with the resolve to tread the spiritual path that history now records. However long it took him to complete his journey is a matter of speculation, but in due course the youngster arrived at a house on the Sablon de Sainte-Gudule, the home of his uncle, where he was warmly received, and where he stayed, evidently with family approval, for many years.

His uncle, a man of independent means, but also of great piety, together with Franco de Coudenberg, a fellow priest and canon, had founded a small mystical association dedicated to the simple life of prayer, and the exercise of charitable works. Within the harmonious environment of this spiritual fraternity, the young Jan van Ruysbroeck waxed strong, and under the guidance of his benefactors received a sound education, not only in theology and philosophy, but also in the religious life. It has been said that he was not always an attentive student, indeed, according to Pomerius,[1] Ruysbroeck showed little inclination for study. This attitude must have changed at some point, for his written works demonstrate not only a profound understanding of the spiritual teachings of the Church, but also a considerable grasp of the natural sciences of his time. Certainly, Gerson, the chancellor of the University of Paris thought so, for in the deed of accusation he drew up against Ruysbroeck's pantheistic ideas, he declared, "It has been said that the man who wrote this book was illiterate and uneducated, and consequently an attempt has been made to regard it as inspired by the Holy Spirit, but this book gives evidence rather of human scholarship..."[2]

---

[1]   Pomerius, *De origine monasterii Viridisvallis una cum vita B. Johannis Rusbrochii.* (Analecta Bollandiana iv., 1885). Pomerius was prior of Ruysbroeck's own community of Groenendael. His life of Ruysbroeck and the foundation of the monastery was finished circa 1420.

[2]   *Epistola . . . ad fr. Bartholomaeum,* in *Gersonii opera* i., p. 59.

As the years passed, Ruysbroeck spent more and more time assisting his uncle in the services of the church. Eventually, in 1317, at the age of twenty-four, he took Holy Orders and in due course was presented with a prebend[3] in St. Gudule's where, for more than twenty-five years, he diligently served as chaplain, exercising his ministry with warmth and compassion, during which time he attained a reputation as a fine preacher and a religious thinker. The most notable element of this period of his life was his conflict with the heretical sect, the Brethren of the Free Spirit,[4] which was one of a number of heretical movements that emerged in the early part of the fourteenth century. This particular sect flourished in the Low Countries. Its members based their doctrine on a pantheistic conception of the Godhead and a perverse interpretation of the "divinity of man," preaching an extreme form of Quietism—a mystical philosophy that

---

Gerson is referring to the third book of *The Adornment of the Spiritual Marriage.*

[3] A stipend or pension, from the revenues of a cathedral, given to a canon.

[4] A later name for an early thirteenth-century sect called the Amalricians, after Amalric of Bena, who, with David of Dinant, taught that God is identical with primal matter, and that there is only one substance, both of body and soul. Their teachings maintained that for those who realized their identity with God, any action whatsoever was permitted, including theft, rape, incest, and murder.

maintains that spiritual perfection can be found only in the complete passivity of the soul. It was the Spaniard Miguel de Molinos who in the seventeenth century developed Quietism into an extreme form. He maintained that man must annihilate his powers and that the desire to do anything actively is offensive to God, and that one must abandon oneself to God. Thus by doing nothing, the soul annihilates itself and returns to its source, in which it is transformed and divinized. In imitation of the Apostles, the exponents of the Brethren of the Free Spirit wandered from place to place, and their teachings spread widely throughout western continental Europe.

One such exponent, a woman named Bloemardinne, was very active and successful in promoting the Brethren's doctrines in the environs of Brussels, particularly through the propagation of pamphlets written in the popular tongue. Ruysbroeck countered Bloemardinne's misinformation by using her methods—circulating pamphlets in the vernacular—to argue against her teachings as false doctrine, and in doing so he was able to marshal the intellectual forces of the city and its environs. However, this made him many enemies; indeed, a campaign was waged against him by her supporters to the extent that he was ridiculed on the streets of Brussels and rude songs were made up about him. This persecution continued for some time, but apparently failed to stop him. Unfortunately, none of these pamphlets have survived, although the spirit of these polemics may be found in some of his writings.[5]

In 1343, Ruysbroeck, now fifty years old, accompanied by his two older companions, Jan Hinckaert and Franco de Coudenberg, departed from Brussels to live the life of hermits in the vale of Groenendael, in the heart of the great forest of Soignes. The hermitage there had been granted to them by John III, Duke of Brabant, who had long respected them for their devout and simple life. Here the three brothers of Hinckaert's mystical association lived undisturbed for another five years. However, this peaceful existence did not last, for the reputation of their simple and holy life drew many followers, and while many came for spiritual guidance and advice, many more came to stay. This unexpected development created problems, some of which had political implications. Consequently, in March 1349, after careful deliberation, the growing mystical association adopted the rule of the Augustinian Canons. Ruysbroeck became the first prior and Coudenberg the first provost, but Jan Hinckaert, concerned that his advancing years might prevent him from fulfilling the role, retired to a cell

---

[5]   See, for example, *The Kingdom of God's Lovers.*

in the forest where he dwelled until his death in May, 1350. Under the government of these good men, the priory of Groenendael became renowned for its holiness.

Undoubtedly the expansive silence of the forest was conducive to Ruysbroeck's quickening inner life. Under the canopy of this great forest all of his major works were written, and all in the dialect of his native district of Brabant. A. Wautier D'Aygalliers, in his book, *Ruysbroeck the Admirable*, relates that "the prior wrote only when he felt illumined by divine grace. Then he buried himself in the shadows of the peaceful forest."[6] He wrote as the Holy Spirit moved him, and to that end he carried a tablet with him wherever he went. It is said that he never committed anything to writing unless moved by the Holy Spirit. When so inspired, he would go out into the forest and wander, often for many hours. Concerning this, one story reports that once he had been absent for many hours, and several of his brethren, worried by his lateness, went looking for him and found him sitting under his favourite tree, rapt in ecstasy and surrounded by a brilliant aura of light. It was then, in the depths of the forest, that Ruysbroeck found the time and solitude

---

[6] A. Wautier D'Aygalliers, *Ruysbroeck the Admirable*, Fred Rothwell, trans. (London and Toronto: J. M. Dent & Sons Ltd., 1925), p. 113.

to give expression to his meditations; herein he communed with the divine, glimpsing what few minds ever dream of, and expressing, with a clarity born of true humility, what he saw of the "vast cycle of creation ever returning to its source and origin."[7]

For the remaining thirty-eight years of his life, Ruysbroeck lived in peaceful tranquillity at Groenendael. These were undoubtedly his most fruitful years. The mystical association, now a strong community of Augustinian Canons, was growing into one of the most influential centres of the spiritual life in the Low Countries, and his fame as a contemplative and spiritual director had spread throughout Europe. People came from many parts of the Christian world seeking his counsel, and his writings were eagerly sought after. Ruysbroeck's influence was felt in many monastic establishments, especially in the Netherlands. It is particularly notable upon the work of Gerhard Groote (1340–1384), and consequently upon the Friends of the Common Life and on the Windesheim School, and upon the Rhineland mystic, Johannes Tauler (1300–1361).[8]

---

[7] D'Aygalliers, *Ruysbroeck*, p. 104.

[8] A native of Deventer, the Netherlands, Goote started the *Devotio Modern* and established both the community of the Friends of Common Life, and the Widesheim School. The Friends of the Common Life were groups of laymen serving the *Devotio Moderna,* the search for personal perfection and charitable works. The Windensheim School was comprised of monastic

Eleven of Ruysbroeck's works have survived in various manuscripts, and all of them, including those of doubtful authenticity, are included in the sixteenth-century Latin translation of Laurentius Surius.[9] The eleven books are as follows: *The Spiritual Tabernacle*—a treatise on the tabernacle of the Israelites as a symbolic model of the spiritual life; *The Twelve Points of True Faith*—a mystical interpretation of the creed; *The Book of the Four Temptations*—an attack on false mysticism; *The Kingdom of God's Lovers*—a description of the mystical life, thought to be his earliest work; *The Adornment of the Spiritual Marriage*—a book of spiritual instruction written as a commentary on the text, "Behold, the bridegroom, cometh; go ye out to meet him"; *The Mirror of Eternal Salvation*—a treatise concerning the mystical doctrine of the Eucharist; *The Seven Cloisters*—a tract concerning the symbolism of the monastic life; *The Seven Degrees of the Ladder of Love*—a text on the soul's ascent to the heights of divine love; *The Book of the Sparkling Stone*—a work

---

communities founded by Gerhard Groote. They were known as the congregation of Windesheim, which became a movement for monastic reform. By circa 1500, it encompassed 97 monasteries. Johannes Tauler was German mystic and disciple of Meister Eckhart, one of the Rhineland Mystics.

[9]   *L. Surius, Joannis Rusbrockii Opera Omnia,* Cologne, 1532. (Surius was a Carthusian monk.)

on the threefold division of man, possibly his finest work; *The Book of Supreme Truth*—a work discussing the three degrees of union with God, in which he also defends himself against the charges of pantheism; *The Twelve Béguines*—possibly his last book, it summarises much of his teaching concerning the spiritual life.

The Adornment of the Spiritual Marriage was written soon after his departure from Brussels. It embodies the essence of his spiritual teaching, a teaching that he developed in divers ways throughout all his books, and deserves careful reflection. Divided into three books, it describes three stages of the spiritual path: the Active, the Contemplative, and the Super-essential Life. In the first book, Ruysbroeck presents us with the beginning of the Active Life. It is a path of purgation and ethical purification.

However, he clearly points out that it is not simply a matter of the soul rejecting the world and turning to God; there is another important part in the equation, and it is this: if the soul is to succeed in its spiritual endeavours, then it is essential that the light of divine grace touch the soul and quicken it.

Ruysbroeck describes this quickening grace as the "Prevenient Grace" of God, which pre-pares the soul for the reception of another, higher light of divine grace—an inward and mysterious working of God that moves the soul and all its powers.

Ruysbroeck teaches that this Prevenient Grace is the first requirement for the quickening of the soul, and through it emerges a second requirement—the free conversion of the will. In this manner, from grace and conversion, love is born, and from love arises a third requirement—the purification of conscience. Thus Ruysbroeck declares,

> . . . God gives His light and by this light man gives his willing and perfect conversion: and of these two is born a perfect love towards God. And from this love there come forth perfect contrition and purification of conscience.[10]

In this quickened state, the soul seeks to purge itself of its old life in the mundane world and to purify the conscience by meditating upon the life of Christ and establishing a new interior life based on His example. Ruysbroeck teaches that we must follow Christ in virtue, the totality of which, in Christ, is both incomprehensible and impossible, but certain virtues are particularly accessible to humanity, these being humility, charity, and patient suffering (fortitude). These, he asserts, are the roots and beginnings of all virtues and all perfection.

In the first virtue, Ruysbroeck draws our attention to the humility of Christ, of which

---

[10] See p. 9 of this volume.

two kinds are exemplified. In the first example,
Ruysbroeck points out that Christ took upon
Himself the nature of man in his fallen state and
chose a poor maiden rather than a king's daughter
for His mother, thereby demonstrating in no
uncertain terms the affinity between humanity
and God. In the second example Ruysbroeck
points out that Christ subjected Himself to the
old law, obeying the laws of Israel, and paying
tribute to Caesar. In this He taught acceptance
as the way to understanding. Thus, Ruysbroeck
teaches us that a humble soul is meek, revering
the Church and the sacraments; is discreet in
food and drink, in speech, behaviour, and dress;
is without hypocrisy or pretence in lowly service;
and is humble in devotion, prostrating the heart
and conscience before God.

In the second virtue, Ruysbroeck draws
our attention to the fact that charity is the
dynamic of love and the beginning and origin
of all virtues. It was love that made Christ stoop
in kindness to the needs of humanity, and in
doing so He gave us a living example, teaching
us by His life how to live ours. Furthermore,
Ruysbroeck declares that Christ fed, "ghostly-
wise," true inward teachings to all who could
understand them; and to others via the senses
with signs and wonders.

In the third virtue, Ruysbroeck draws our
attention to the patient suffering of Christ

throughout His incarnation, declaring that
Christ's suffering began early—with poverty
and cold; that he shed blood in circumcision,
and was driven into exile in a strange country.
Furthermore, that He laboured as a carpenter
to serve His earthly family; that He was taken
prisoner and suffered hunger, thirst, and shame,
was mocked, insulted, scourged, beaten, and
condemned by false witness; that His head was
covered in thorns, and He was eventually nailed
to the cross and pierced with a spear.

Thus, Ruysbroeck taught that the practice of
these virtues prepares the soul for the coming of
Christ. Having established these virtues as the
basis for the new life of the soul, Ruysbroeck
addresses the life of Christ in the soul, which he
declares takes place every day within good souls—
each according to its power and ability. Thus,
when a soul takes a stand in its own smallness
and truly confesses its poverty and helplessness, it
becomes more radiant and enlightened by grace,
more ardent in love, and more fruitful in perfect
virtues and good works. In this the soul learns
to "Behold" Christ in all things, to recognise
that when He incarnated as man and lived in
humility among us and died for us, He set an
example that we should imitate by exercising
the perfect moral virtues of charity and humility,
and furthermore, that we should never forget
that He is ever-present and always comes with

grace to each loving heart, and for this coming we should long and pray daily. Ruysbroeck emphasises time and time again that a soul should always stretch toward God with love. This is, according to Ruysbroeck, the "going out to meet God." He declares that,

> In this way, and in this wise we should go out to meet Christ with an upright intention during all our lives, and in all our works, and in all our virtues; so that we may also meet Him in the light of glory at the hour of death.
>
> This method and this way of which you have now heard, is called the Active Life. It is needful for all men.[11]

In this way a soul, who learns through patience and perseverance to live this life in its perfection, will be driven to know Christ in himself. To accomplish this, the soul must climb the Tree of Faith, a tree that grows downward, and whose roots are in the Godhead. This tree, Ruysbroeck declares (Book I, chapter 12), has twelve branches. The lower branches speak of those things which belong to our salvation, while the upper branches tell of God, of the Trinity, and of the unity and nature of God.

---

[11] See p. 46 of this volume.

> The soul must cling to that "unity" in
> the highest parts of the tree; for there it
> is that Jesus must pass with all His gifts.
> When the soul climbs with desire above
> the multiplicity of creatures, and above
> the works of the senses, and above the light
> of nature then it meets Christ in the light
> of Faith, and becomes enlightened.[12]

Thus ends the first book.

The language of Ruysbroeck is easily taken for granted, but we should note that it is not always to be taken at face value. He speaks in the *lingua franca* of medieval mysticism. It is a poetic language that conceals as much as it reveals, and requires a great deal of reflection before it discloses its message. This is most immediately apparent in the second book wherein Ruysbroeck addresses the Contemplative Life, drawing on the parable of the wise and foolish virgins (Matt. 25:1–10). He likens a wise virgin to a soul who has abandoned the ways of the mundane world and learned, as described in the first book, to live according to the virtues of God. Drawing on the parable further he declares, quoting the scriptures, that when the soul becomes drowsy and inert,

> Then, at midnight, when it is least
> expected, a ghostly cry is made within the
> soul: BEHOLD, THE BRIDEGROOM,

---

[12] See p. 48 of this volume.

COMETH, GO YE OUT TO MEET
HIM. Of this beholding, and of the inward
coming of Christ, and of man's ghostly
going out, and of his meeting with Christ,
of these four points we will now speak.[13]

Ruysbroeck informs us that by these words
Christ teaches us four important things, first:
BEHOLD—that our understanding should
be enlightened by a supernatural light, the
light of Divine Grace, and this in a more lofty
degree than hitherto experienced. Second: THE
BRIDEGROOM, COMETH—that Christ will
show us what we ought to see; namely, Eternal
Truth symbolised by the "inward coming of the
bridegroom." Third: GO YE OUT TO MEET
HIM—that we should go out by inward exercises
according to righteousness; exercises that cast
out all distracting images and attachments
from the heart; that the soul may be free and
imageless, released from all attachments and
empty of all creatures. Fourth—that the aim
and end of the whole is the meeting with the
Christ in the unity of the Godhead.

This important instruction is given as a
guide to the soul in its ascent of the Tree of
Faith referred to at the end of the first book.
Ruysbroeck is teaching those who have the eyes
to see that the light of the mundane world,

---

[13] See p. 50 of this volume.

which is the light of inferior reason, cannot
illuminate the deeper spiritual recesses of the
soul, and therefore cannot fathom the profound
nature of reality. Yet, in the depths of prayer
and meditation, the inferior reason together
with all that is associated with it, passes away.
Ruysbroeck alludes to this passing when he
draws on the scriptural reference of the virgins
becoming drowsy and falling asleep (Matt. 25:
5). Furthermore, he states that this sleep is an
indication of the dawning of a new spiritual
awareness—in his words, "a supernatural
light," which heralds an emerging spiritual
consciousness of the Eternal Truth, which, in
other words, is "Reality." This is in many ways
only the beginning of his teaching, for the first
book is dedicated to the work of the novice,
hence the reference to the Active Life. It is a
life that leads the aspiring soul to the threshold
of the mystical life—a life of an inner reality.
Such a life is a process of continually growing
in the presence of the Divine, a process that
Ruysbroeck calls the Contemplative Life.

The first chapters of the second book are
rich mines of perfect spiritual insight concerning
the mystical ascent of the soul. Here, those
who would establish their consciousness in the
presence of God are instructed to cast out all
distracting images and attachments from the
heart, and the mind, and to direct the will

toward gathering together all of the faculties and powers of the soul, for then, and only then, does the concentrated will flow into the Unity of God and into the Unity of Mind.

Furthermore, Ruysbroeck instructs the aspiring contemplative to understand the threefold unity of the soul. He emphasises that the first and highest unity of the soul is in God; that the second unity is a unity of our higher powers and that the third unity rests in the unity of the heart, which is the unity of all bodily powers, including the senses. These three unities abide in the soul as one life and one kingdom. In the lowest, we are sensible and animal; in the middle, we are rational and spiritual; and in the highest, we are according to our essence.

His teaching on this subject is not so far removed from the teachings of Plotinus and his followers, although the context is very different. In the teachings of Plotinus it is the aspiring soul that must accomplish the ascent through the power of the will—and that in a most subtle manner—but Ruysbroeck clearly follows the way of St. Paul and the Pseudo-Dionysius, in that the ascent is accomplished not through the power of the will but through the power of the Holy Spirit acting upon the soul. This power, in itself a mystery to the human mind, is the Pre-venient Grace referred to in the first book, and which is experienced by the soul as the presence of the love of God, a presence that emerges, not at our behest, but of its own accord, although it comes in response, so it would seem, to the prayers of those who are truly humble. This grace acts as a quickening agent upon the soul, and until that quickening has taken place, then no act of will, however strong or knowledgeable of rites and incantations, will ever open the doors of the spiritual world.

For those who are prepared to do the work the path is then made clear. The lowest unity is perfected through outward works and moral perfection, a path undertaken through the quickening power of the Prevenient Grace of God. This is the way of the Active Life. The second or middle unity is the way of the Contemplative. It is perfected supernaturally through the inflow of grace and the application of the three virtues—faith, hope, and charity—concerning which Ruysbroeck has dedicated these books.

The third and highest unity is the way of the Super-essential Life; it is above the comprehension of reason, yet it is essentially within us. This Super-essential Life is perfected in the deeper understanding of the work of love, which rests, inevitably, in the heart of God; from here the grace of God pours into the soul, from "within" and not from without, for God is more inward to us than we are to ourselves. Here the soul learns to "abide" in the ever-present love of God, and in the light of that eternal sun to fulfil the divine potential that has ever resided within. This is nowhere better illustrated than in chapter sixty-four of the second book, titled "Of the Highest Degree of the Most Interior Life":

> Now understand this well: that measureless splendour of God, which together with the incomprehensible brightness, is the cause of all gifts and of all virtues—that same Uncomprehended Light transfigures the fruitive tendency of our spirit and penetrates it in a way that is wayless; that is, through the Uncomprehended Light. And in this light the spirit immerses itself in fruitive rest; for this rest is wayless and fathomless, and one can know of it in no other way than through itself—that is through rest. For, could we know and comprehend it, it would fall into mode and measure; then it could not satisfy us, but rest would become an eternal restlessness. And for this reason, the simple, loving and immersed tendency of our spirit works within us a fruitive love; and this fruitive love is abysmal. And the abyss of God calls to the abyss; that is, of all those who are united with the Spirit of God in fruitive love. This inward call is an inundation of the essential brightness, . . . enfolding us in an abysmal love, causing us to be lost to ourselves, and to flow forth from ourselves into the wild darkness of the Godhead.[14]

---

[14] See page 149 of this volume.

Here we may easily recognise just how great the influence of the Pseudo-Dionysius was on Ruysbroeck's thought. Indeed, there are moments when it is difficult to distinguish between the two authors; consider the following extract from the *Mystical Theology* of Dionysius and compare it with the above:

> Unto this darkness which is beyond light we pray that we may come, and may attain unto vision through the loss of sight and knowledge, and that in ceasing thus to see and to know we may learn to know that which is beyond all perception and understanding . . . and that we may offer Him that transcends all things the praises of a transcendent hymnody, which we shall do by denying or removing all things that are—like as men who, carving a statue out of marble, remove all the impediments that hinder the clear perceptive of the latent image and by this mere removal display the hidden statue itself in its hidden beauty.[15]

Undoubtedly there is a connection between them, but it is not merely one of literary or intellectual familiarity; rather, it is the inherent affinity that is forged between souls that have drunk from the same well of inspiration; both

[15] *Dionysius the Areopagite on the Divine Names and The Mystical Theology*. C. E. Rolt, trans. (Berwick, ME: Ibis Press, 2004), p. 194.

speak the same strange language born of personal experience, although the best part of a thousand years separate them.

That Ruysbroeck was so greatly influenced by Dionysius should come as no surprise, for the Dionysian corpus has influenced many of our civilisation's great minds. This was particularly so of the fourteenth century, where the Neo-Platonism of the great Dominicans—Thomas Aquinas, Albertus Magnus, and Meister Eckhart, all of whom were influenced to some degree by Dionysius—was very much present in the intellectual landscape of Europe. Thomas Aquinas, perhaps the most celebrated luminary of medieval scholasticism, wrote commentaries on the Dionysian corpus, as did Albertus Magnus, and doubtless some of these commentaries came into Ruysbroeck's hands. Meister Eckhart, who acquired the title of *lector biblicus* while teaching at the University of Paris, and who in his later years taught and preached at Cologne, explicitly draws upon Dionysius, particularly with reference to the divine Nothingness, and is certainly one of the greatest exponents of the Dionysian *Via Negativa,* the path of absolute imageless transcendence. It is this path, of which Ruysbroeck is so obviously an authority, that is central to the spiritual teachings of so many of the great Christian mystics.[16]

---

[16] Albertus Magnus, or Albert the Great (ca. 1206–1280), was

It is generally accepted that there is a connection between Ruysbroeck and Eckhart, and
there is obviously a similarity in their teachings,
but there is no clear evidence of any direct personal association, although tradition tells of a visit
Ruysbroeck made to Cologne, where it is said he
heard Eckhart speak and was deeply impressed
by him. Whether they actually met matters
little, as copies of Eckhart's sermons were readily
available, especially to a cathedral chaplain such as
Ruysbroeck, who would have come across some of
them in the course of his official duties. It is worth
bearing in mind when considering these things
that Ruysbroeck was not only a contemplative
but also a dedicated churchman who functioned
in a professional capacity for more than twenty-
five years; and as such he would have considered
it part of his duty to be informed about what was
taking place in the world around him. However,
if he was influenced at all, it was by more than

---

one of the first Dominicans to write on spiritual theology,
and played a significant role in the momentous intellectual
developments of the thirteenth century. Meister Eckhart (ca.
1260–1327) was a learned member of the Dominican order,
and sometime *lector biblicus* at the University of Paris where
he acquired his title of "Meister" by Pope Boniface VIII. He
graduated, probably at Cologne, in the scholasticism of Albertus
Magnus and Thomas Aquinas, and held important provincial
posts. But it was principally in Strassburg and Cologne that
he established his reputation for being a great teacher and
the "father of the German language."

one person and from more than one source, and
apart from those luminaries already mentioned
we should also include many of the early Church
Fathers, especially the great St. Augustine, not
to mention John Scotus Erigena, St. Bernard of
Clairvaux, and the Victorines.[17] In fact, it could
be said that they all combined to serve as an
influence upon the intellectual life of Ruysbroeck,
for they were all to some degree conduits of the
Christian mystical tradition. Yet, regardless of his
metaphysical credentials, one thing is absolutely
clear; Ruysbroeck was first and foremost a
Christian. . At the heart of everything, what he
taught and wrote were the teachings of Christ. The
great commandment, "Thou shalt love the Lord
thy God with all thy heart, and with all thy soul,
and with all thy strength, and with all thy mind
and thy neighbour as thy self" (Luke 10:27) was
engraved upon his heart. Love was the central
pivot upon which his entire life was balanced; this
is the central theme of all his major works, and
upon which his greatness rests.

In *The Book of the Sparkling Stone,* Ruysbroeck
declares that,

---

[17] The Victorines were a small order with great intellectual
influence. The monastery had many students, and in the 13th
century it became a college within the University of Paris. In
the following century, the monastery began to decline, and in
the 15th century, the monks joined the Brotherhood of the
Common Life, founded in Holland.

> [W]hen we transcend ourselves, and
> become, in our ascent towards God, so
> simple that the naked love in the height
> can lay hold of us, where love enfolds
> love, above every exercise of virtue—
> that is, in our Origin, of which we are
> spiritually born—then we cease, and we
> and all selfhood die in God. (p. 202)

This love is a love that is beyond the control of the wilful soul; in fact, it is a love that is neither the gift of an individual nor the gift of humanity. It is in *fine* the gift of God. We may desire it and even strive for it, but it is not ours to give or to do with as we will. This is an important consideration for aspiring contemplatives, who, in the weakness of apparent successes in the mystical life, do not recognise that inspiration, filtering through the dense mass of worldly sensation, leads the soul as a light moving in the dark leads the unsuspecting moth.

Thus, in the alembic of the mind, the true source of inspiration is obscured by the dancing thoughts, images, and sensations that lead the overconfident soul in a merry dance of either trying to "think it out" and thereby control the situation, or to embody a naive conception of what may pass for spiritual love, and in a well-meaning conceit parade before the world as if enlightened. This conceit is a pitfall all souls must overcome, if they are to attain the highest goal, for the way to spiritual enlightenment is not through a refined ensemble of faculties. It is, rather, as defined by Ruysbroeck, attained through the total application of being and at every level, although not necessarily concurrently. This he addresses in one way or another throughout *The Adornment of the Spiritual Marriage,* which, when looked at from another perspective, may be seen as a technical manual for the mystical life, which indeed it is. However, his language is the language of the medieval Christian mystic, but make no mistake, his words, although veiled from the profane, contain every bit as much, and more, that one might expect from volumes purported to be the works of angels and ascended masters. In one of his other books, *The Twelve Béguines,* he wrote:

> Those who follow the way of love
> Are the richest of all men living:
> They are bold, frank and fearless,
> They have neither travail nor care,
> For the Holy Ghost bears all their burdens.
> They seek no outward seeming,
> They desire nought that is esteemed of men,
> They affect not singular conduct,
> They would be like other good men.

For those who are able to penetrate beyond the picturesque and sometimes archaic constructs of his language, and perceive that which is hidden beneath, there is the satisfaction of discovering the true inner life of the soul. It is a marvellous world of spiritual reality impervious to the acquisitive nature of inferior reason, which will never gain access to it. The only thing that any aspirant can do to gain entrance to this world is follow the words of Christ: "Sell all that you have . . . and come, follow me" (Luke 18:22). In his own way, Ruysbroeck taught this. For more than thirty years he was celebrated as a spiritual director, not so much for his rhetoric and philosophical insight, but for his ability to convey a sense of the numinous in which restless souls might for a moment experience "the peace that mankind can neither give nor take away"; and therein learn what it means to "give up all." This was his work and his life. He lived it through and through, and he shared it with his fellow canons and those in his spiritual care.

For much of his time at Groenendael, Ruysbroeck lived the quiet life of a hermit, and although he was the spiritual director of many he knew that he would never be able to reach all of the souls who were seeking spiritual direction, and so he composed the works for which he is now renowned. His works speak for themselves; they are a tribute to the life of one who obediently followed the guidance of the Holy Spirit. His sense of individuality, so important to us who live in the modern world, was sublimated into a life of service and thereby became a living example to all around him. He demonstrated that the personality born of the experience of the mundane world counts for very little until it is put into service for the spiritual betterment of humanity. His influence upon Gerhard de Groote and the Brethren of the Common Life, and subsequently upon the course of the Reformation, has yet to be fully evaluated. The same may be said of his influence upon other strands of Christian mystical endeavour that are still percolating throughout the fabric of human consciousness today.

D'Aygalliers reports that one night Ruysbroeck's mother appeared before him, announcing that Advent would not pass without God receiving His old servant back to Himself. Thus forewarned, Ruysbroeck arranged to be taken into the common infirmary. No sooner had he been carried there than he succumbed to a fever. Two weeks later, on the second of December, 1381, he called the brothers to him, commended himself to their memory and, smiling at them, passed away. It is said that at the same moment Gerhard de Groote knew of Ruysbroeck's death and that the bells of Deventer began to ring on their own. He appeared in visions to those of his disciples who undertook to bury the body of "the sweetest monastic flower."

Considered to be the foremost of the Flemish mystics, the Blessed John Ruysbroeck was beatified on the 1st of December, 1908, by Pope Pius X. His canonisation is pending. He is also known, variously, as the Admirable Doctor and the Divine Doctor. There is no known authentic portrait of the Blessed John Ruysbroeck, however, he is invariably represented in canonical habit, seated in the forest with his writing tablet upon his lap, rapt in ecstasy and enveloped in flames, without consuming the tree under which he is resting.

"My words," said Ruysbroeck "are strange, but those who love will understand."

Allan Armstrong
Prior of
the Order of
Dionysis & Paul
January 2005

THE ADORNMENT
OF THE SPIRITUAL MARRIAGE

THE FIRST BOOK

PROLOGUE

Ecce sponsus venit,
exite obviam ei.

BEHOLD, THE BRIDEGROOM COMETH, GO YE OUT TO
MEET HIM. These words were written by St Matthew
the Evangelist, and Christ spoke them to His disciples
and to all other men in the parable of the virgins.
This Bridegroom is Christ, and human nature is the
bride ; the which God has made in His own image
and after His likeness. And in the beginning He had
set her in the highest and most beautiful, the richest
and most fertile place in all the earth : that is, in
Paradise. And He had given her dominion over all
creatures ; and He had adorned her with graces ;
and had given her a commandment, so that by
obedience she might have merited to be confirmed
and established with her Bridegroom in an eternal
troth, and never to fall into any grief, or any sin.

Then came a beguiler, the hellish fiend, full of envy,
in the shape of a subtle serpent, and he beguiled the
woman ; and they both beguiled the man, in whom
above all the whole of our nature consists. And the
fiend seduced that nature, the bride of God, with false
counsel ; and she was driven into a strange country,

poor and miserable and captive and oppressed, and
beset by her enemies ; so that it seemed as though
she might never attain reconciliation and return again
to her native land.

But when God thought the time had come, and had
mercy on the suffering of His beloved, He sent His
Only Begotten Son to earth, in a fair chamber, in a
glorious temple ; that is, in the body of the Virgin
Mary. There He was married to this bride, our
nature, and He united her with His own person
through the most pure blood of this noble Virgin.
The priest who married the bride was the Holy
Ghost ; the angel Gabriel brought the offer ; the
glorious Virgin gave her consent. Thus Christ, our
faithful Bridegroom, united our nature with His
person ; and He has sought us in strange countries,
and taught us heavenly customs and perfect faithfulness, and has laboured for us and fought as our
champion against the adversary. And He has broken
open our prison, and won the victory, and by His
death slain our death ; and He has redeemed us by
His blood, and made us free through His living waters
of baptism, and enriched us with His sacraments
and with His gifts : that we might go out (as He says)
with all the virtues, to meet Him in the house of glory,
and to enjoy Him without end in eternity.

Now Christ, the Master of Truth, says : BEHOLD
THE BRIDEGROOM COMETH, GO YE OUT TO MEET HIM.
In these words, Christ our Lover teaches us four
things. First, He gives us a command, in that He
says : BEHOLD. Those who neglect this command
and remain blind are all damned. Secondly, He
shows us what we shall see, that is, the coming of
the Bridegroom ; for He says, THE BRIDEGROOM

COMETH. In the third place, He teaches and commands us what we shall do, for He says : Go ye out. And in the fourth place, by saying : To meet Him, He shows us the use and the purpose of our labour and of all our life; that is to say, the loving meeting with our Bridegroom.

These words we shall now declare and set forth in three ways. First, according to the common way relating to the life of beginners, which is called the Active Life, and which is necessary for all men who wish to be saved. Secondly, we will explain these same words in their relation to the interior, exalted, and God-desiring life, at which many men may arrive by their virtues and by the grace of God. Thirdly, we will expound them in respect of a super-essential, God-seeing life, which few men can attain or taste, by reason of the sublimity and high nobility of that life.

CHAPTER I

OF THE ACTIVE LIFE

Since the time of Adam, Christ, the Wisdom of the Father, has said to all men, and He says so still, inwardly according to His Divinity : Behold. And this beholding is needful. Now mark this well : that for anyone who wishes to see, either in a bodily or a ghostly manner, three things are necessary.

The first thing is that, if a man will see bodily and outwardly, he must have the outward light of heaven, or some other material light, to illuminate the medium, that is, the air, through which he will see. The second thing is, that he must permit the things which he wishes to see to be reflected in his eyes. And the third thing is that the organs, the eyes, must be sound and flawless, so that gross bodily things can be subtly reflected in them. If a man lack any of these three things his bodily sight is wanting. Of this sight, however, we shall say nothing more ; but we shall speak of a ghostly and supernatural sight, in which all our bliss abides.

For all who wish to see in a ghostly and supernatural manner three things also are needful. The first is the light of Divine grace ; the second is a free turning of the will to God ; the third is a conscience clean from any mortal sin.

Now mark this : God being a common good, and His boundless love being common to all, He gives His grace in two ways : prevenient grace, and the grace by which one merits eternal life. Prevenient grace is common to all men, Pagan and Jew, good and evil. By reason of His common love, which God has towards all men, He has caused His name and the redemption of human nature to be preached and revealed to the uttermost parts of the earth. Whosoever wishes to turn to Him can turn to Him. All the sacraments, baptism and every other sacrament, are made ready for all men who wish to receive them, according to the needs of each ; for God wishes to save all men and to lose not one. At the day of Judgment, no one shall be able to complain that, had he wished to be converted, but little was done for him. Thus God is a common light and a common splendour, enlightening heaven and earth, and every man, each according to his need and worth.

But although, even as God is common to all, the sun shines upon all trees, yet many a tree remains without fruits, and many a tree brings forth wild fruits of little use to men. And for this reason such trees are pruned, and shoots of fruitful trees are grafted into them, so that they may bear good fruits, savoury and useful to man.

The light of Divine grace is a fruit-bearing shoot, coming forth from the living paradise of the eternal kingdom ; and no deed can bring refreshment or profit to man if it be not born of this shoot. This shoot of Divine grace, which makes man pleasing to God, and through which he merits eternal life, is offered to all men. But it is not grafted into all, because some will not cut away the wild branches of their trees ; that is, unbelief, and a perverse and disobedient will opposed to the commandments of God.

But if this shoot of God's grace is to be grafted into our souls, there must be of necessity three things : the prevenient grace of God, the conversion of one's own free will, and the purification of conscience. The prevenient grace touches all men, God bestowing it upon all men. But not all men give on their part the conversion of the will and the purification of conscience ; and that is why so many lack the grace of God, through which they should merit eternal life.

The prevenient grace of God touches a man from without and from within. From without through sickness ; or through the loss of external goods, of kinsmen, and of friends ; or through public disgrace. Or he may be stirred by a sermon, or by the examples of the saints or of good men, their words, or their deeds ; so that he learns to recognize himself as he is. This is how God touches a man from without.

Sometimes a man is touched also from within, through remembering the sorrows and the sufferings of our Lord, and the good which God has bestowed upon him and upon all other men ; or by considering his sins, the shortness of life, the fear of death and the fear of hell, the eternal torments of hell and the eternal joy of heaven, and how God has spared him in his sins and has awaited his conversion. Or he may ponder the marvellous works of God in heaven and in earth, and in all creatures. Such are the workings of the prevenient grace of God, stirring men from without and from within, in many ways. And besides this, man has a natural tendency towards God, because of the spark of the soul, and because of that highest reason, which always desires the good and hates the evil. In all these ways God touches all men, each one according to his need ; so that at times a man is smitten, reproved, alarmed, and stands still within himself to consider himself. And all this is still prevenient grace, and not yet efficacious grace. Thus does prevenient grace prepare the soul for the reception of the other grace, through which eternal life is merited. For when the soul has thus got rid of evil willing and evil doing, it is perplexed and smitten with fear of what it should do, considering itself, its wicked works, and God. And from this there arise a natural repentance of its sins and a natural good-will. Such is the highest work of prevenient grace.

If a man does all he can, and cannot do more because of his feebleness, it rests with the infinite goodness of God to finish the work. Then, straight as a sunbeam, there comes a higher light of Divine grace, and it is shed into the soul according to its worth, though neither merited nor desired. For in this light God gives Himself out of free goodness and generosity, the which never creature can merit before it has received it. And this is an inward and mysterious working of God in the soul, above time ; and it moves the soul and all its powers. Therewith ends prevenient grace and begins the other grace, that is to say, the supernatural light.

This light is the first point necessary, and from it there arises a second point, and that on the part of the soul ; namely, the free conversion of the will, in a single moment of time. And here it is that charity is born of the union of God with the soul. These two points hang together, so that the one cannot be fulfilled without the other. Where God and the soul come together in the union of love, then God, above time, gives His light ; and the soul, in a single moment of time, gives, by virtue of the grace received, its free conversion to Him. And there charity is born of God and of the soul in the soul, for charity is a bond of love, tying God to the loving soul.

Of these two things—that is to say, the grace of God and the free conversion of the will enlightened by grace—charity, that is, Divine love, is born. And from this Divine love the third point arises ; that is, the purification of conscience. And these three points belong together in such a way that one cannot exist long without the others ; for whosoever has Divine love has also perfect contrition for his sins.

Yet here we must take heed to the order of Divine and creaturely things as they are here shown. For God gives His light, and by this light man gives his willing and perfect conversion : and of these two is born a perfect love towards God. And from this love there come forth perfect contrition and purification of conscience. And these arise from the consideration of misdeeds and all that may defile the soul :

for when a man loves God he despises himself and all his works. This is the order of every conversion. From it there come true repentance, a perfect sorrow for every evil thing which one has done, and an ardent desire never to sin again and evermore to serve God in humble obedience. Hence too an open confession, without reserve, ambiguity, or excuse ; a perfect satisfaction according to the counsel of a prudent priest ; and the beginning of virtue and of all good works.

These three things, as you have heard, are needful to a spiritual or godly sight. If you have them, Christ is saying within you : BEHOLD, and you are beholding in truth. And this is the first of the four chief points ; namely, that in which Christ our Lord says : BEHOLD.

CHAPTER II

SHOWING HOW WE SHALL CONSIDER THE COMING OF CHRIST IN THREE WAYS

Now, by saying : THE BRIDEGROOM COMETH, He shows us further what we shall see. Christ, our Bridegroom, spoke this word in Latin : VENIT. And this word implies two tenses, the past and the present ; and yet here it denotes the future too.

And that is why we shall consider three comings of our Bridegroom, Jesus Christ. In the first coming He became man, for man's sake, out of love. The second coming takes place daily, often and many times, in every loving heart, with new graces and with new gifts, as each is able to receive them. The third coming we shall see as the coming in the Judgment, or at the hour of death. And in all these comings there are three things to be considered : the why and the wherefore, the inward way, and the outward work.

The reason why God created the angels and man, was His unfathomable goodness and nobleness whereby He willed to do it ; that the bliss and the richness which He is Himself might be revealed to rational creatures, so that they might taste Him in time, and enjoy Him outside time in eternity

The reason why God became man was His incomprehensible love, and the need of all men ; for man had been corrupted by the Fall, and could not amend himself.

But the reason why Christ, according to His Godhead and according to His manhood, wrought all His works on earth, this reason is fourfold : His Divine love which is without measure ; the created love, called charity, which He had in His soul through union with the Eternal Word and through the perfect gift of His Father ; the great need of man ; and the glory of His Father. These are the reasons for the coming of Christ our Bridegroom, and for all His works, both outward and inward.

Now, if we would follow Christ our Bridegroom in virtue, so far as we are able, we must consider in what wise He was inwardly and the works which He wrought outwardly ; that is to say, His virtues and the deeds of these virtues.

In what wise He was according to His Godhead, this is inaccessible and incomprehensible to us ; for it is that according to which He is born of the Father without ceasing, and wherein the Father,

in Him and through Him, knows, creates, orders and
rules all things in heaven and on earth. For He is
the Wisdom of the Father, and they breathe forth one
Spirit, that is, one Love, which is a common bond
between Them and all saints, and all good men in
heaven and on earth. Of this condition we shall not
speak any more ; but we shall speak of that condition
which He had through Divine gifts and according
to His created manhood.   And this condition was
manifold.   For as many inward virtues as Christ
possessed, so many were His inward conditions : for
every virtue has its special condition. The sum of
the virtues and conditions in the soul of Christ,
this is above the understanding and above the comprehension of all creatures.   But we shall take three
of them : namely, humility, charity, and patient
suffering, in inward and outward things.   These are
the three chief roots and beginnings of all virtues
and all perfection.

CHAPTER III

OF HUMILITY

Now understand this : we find in Christ, according
to His Godhead, two kinds of humility.
    The first kind is this : that He willed to become
man, and took upon Himself that very nature which
had been banished and cursed to the bottom of hell,
and willed to become one with it according to His
personality ; so that now any man, either good or
evil, can say : Christ, the Son of God, is my brother.
    The second kind of humility according to His
Godhead consists in this ; that He chose a poor

maiden, and not a king's daughter, for His mother, so that a poor maiden should be the mother of God, who is Lord of heaven and earth and all creatures.

And further, we can say of all the works of humility which Christ ever wrought, that they were wrought by God Himself.

Now let us take the humility which was in Christ according to His manhood and through the grace and the gifts of God. In this humility His soul with all its powers bowed down in reverence and adoration before the most high might of the Father ; for a bowed down heart is a humble heart. And therefore He wrought all His works for the praise and for the honour of His Father, and never and in nothing sought His own glory according to His humanity.

He was humble and subject to the old law, and to the commandments, and also to custom whenever such was right. And that is why He was circumcised, and taken into the temple, and redeemed in the customary way ; and He paid His tribute money to Cæsar like any other Jew. And He was humble and subject to His mother and to the lord Joseph ; and that is why He served them with true reverence according to all their needs. He chose poor and outcast people for His comrades, to live with, and wherewith to convert the world : these were the Apostles. And He was lowly and meek among them and among all other men. And He was ever ready for all men in whatever inward or outward need they might be : as if he were the servant of all the world.

This is the first point which we find in Christ our Bridegroom.

CHAPTER IV

OF CHARITY

THE second point is charity, beginning and origin of all virtues. This charity upheld the higher powers of His soul in quietness, and in a fruition of that very bliss which He now enjoys. And this charity kept Him constantly uplifted to His Father in reverence, in love, in adoration, in praise ; with fervent prayers for the needs of all men, and with an offering up of all His works to the glory of His Father.

It was also this same charity that made Christ stoop with loving faithfulness and kindness to the bodily and ghostly needs of all men. And in this He gave an example to all men, teaching them by His life how to live. He fed in ghostly wise with true and inward teachings all those men who could understand them : and others from without through the senses with signs and wonders. And sometimes He fed them also with bodily food, as when they had followed Him into the desert and were in need of it. He made the deaf hear and the lame walk straight, and the blind see, and the dumb speak, and cast forth devils from men. He raised up the dead ; and this should be understood both in a bodily and a ghostly way. Christ, our Lover, has laboured for us from without and from within, with true faithfulness. His charity we cannot fathom and understand, for it flows out of the unfathomable fountain of the Holy Ghost, and transcends all that creatures have ever experienced of charity ; for Christ was God and man in one Person.

And this is the second point : that is to say, charity.

CHAPTER V

OF PATIENT ENDURANCE

THE third point is patient endurance. We should mark this point carefully, for it adorned Christ our Bridegroom during all His life. For His sufferings began very early, as soon as He was born ; they began with poverty and cold. Then He was circumcised and shed His blood ; He was driven to a strange country ; He served the lord Joseph and His mother ; He suffered hunger and thirst, shame and contempt, the vile words and works of the Jews. He fasted, He watched, and He was tempted by the devil. He was subject to all men ; He wandered from country to country, from town to town, with much labour and great zeal, that He might preach the Gospel.

At last He was taken prisoner by the Jews, who were His enemies, though He was their friend. He was betrayed, mocked and insulted, scourged and buffetted, and condemned by false witness. He bore His cross with great pains up to the highest point of the land. He was stripped stark naked. So fair a body neither man nor woman ever saw so cruelly ill-used. He suffered shame, and anguish, and cold, before all the world : for He was naked, and it was cold, and a searching wind cut into His wounds. He was nailed to the wood of the cross with blunt nails, and so stretched out that His veins were torn asunder. He was lifted up and then flung down, and because of the blow His wounds began to bleed again. His head was crowned with thorns ; His ears heard the Jews cry in their fury : CRUCIFY HIM, CRUCIFY HIM, with many other infamous words. His eyes saw the hardness and malice of the Jews, and the anguish of His mother. And His eyes overflowed with the bitterness of sorrow and death ; His nose smelt the filth which the Jews spat out of their mouths into His face ; His mouth and tongue dripped with vinegar mingled with gall, and every sensitive part of His body had been wounded by the scourge.

Christ our Bridegroom, wounded to the death, forsaken of God and of all creatures, dying on the cross, hanging like a log for which no one cared, save Mary, His poor mother, who could not help Him !

Christ also suffered spiritually, in His soul, because of the hardened hearts of the Jews and of those who were putting Him to death ; for whatever signs and wonders they saw, they remained in their wickedness. And He suffered because of their corruption and because of the vengeance for His death ; for He knew that God would avenge it on them, body and soul. Also He suffered from the distress and anguish of His mother and His disciples, who were in great affliction. And He suffered still more, because His death would be of no profit to so many men, and because of the ingratitude of man and because of the false oaths which many would swear, reviling and blaspheming Him Who had died out of love for us all. And also His bodily nature and His lower reason suffered, because God had withdrawn the inflow of His grace and of His consolations, and had left them alone in such distress. And of this Christ complained, exclaiming : MY GOD, MY GOD, WHY HAST THOU FORSAKEN ME ? But as to all His sufferings our Lover was silent ; and cried to His Father saying : FATHER, FORGIVE THEM ; FOR THEY KNOW NOT WHAT THEY DO. And Christ was heard of His Father because of His reverence; for those who acted from ignorance were soon afterwards converted.

These then were Christ's inward virtues: humility, charity, and patient endurance. These three virtues Christ our Bridegroom practised during all His life, and He died with them, and paid our debt according to justice. And of His generosity He has opened His side. Thence flow forth the rivers of well-being and the sacraments of bliss. And He has ascended in power, and sits at the right hand of the Father, and reigns in eternity.

This is the first coming of our Bridegroom, and it is wholly past.

CHAPTER VI

OF THE SECOND COMING OF CHRIST

THE second coming of Christ our Bridegroom takes place every day within good men; often and many times, with new graces and gifts, in all those who make themselves ready for it, each according to his power. We would not speak here of a man's first conversion, nor of the first grace which was given to him when he turned from sin to the virtues. But we would speak of an increase of new gifts and new virtues from day to day, and of the present coming of Christ our Bridegroom which takes place daily within our souls.

Now we must consider the why and the wherefore, the way and the working of this coming. Its wherefore is fourfold: God's mercy and our destitution, God's generosity and our desire. These four things cause the growth of virtue and of nobleness.

Now understand this: when the sun sends its beams and its radiance into a deep valley between two high mountains, and, standing in the zenith, can yet shine upon the bottom and ground of the valley, then three things happen: the valley becomes full of light by reflection from the mountains, and it receives more heat, and becomes more fruitful, than the plain and level country. And so likewise, when a good man takes his stand upon his own littleness, in the most lowly part of himself, and confesses and knows that he has nothing, and is nothing, and can nothing, of himself, neither stand still nor go on, and when he sees how often he fails in virtues and good works: then he confesses his poverty and his helplessness, then he makes a valley of humility. And when he is thus humble, and needy, and knows his own need; he lays his distress, and complains of it, before the bounty and the mercy of God. And so he marks the sublimity of God and his own lowliness; and thus he becomes a deep valley. And Christ is a Sun of righteousness and also of mercy, Who stands in the highest part of the firmament, that is, on the right hand of the Father, and from thence He shines into the bottom of the humble heart; for Christ is always moved by helplessness, whenever a man complains of it and lays it before Him with humility. Then there arise two mountains, that is, two desires; one to serve God and praise Him with reverence, the other to attain noble virtues. Those two mountains are higher than the heavens, for these longings touch God without intermediary, and crave His ungrudging generosity. And then that generosity cannot withhold itself, it must flow forth; for then the soul is made ready to receive, and to hold, more gifts.

These are the wherefore, and the way of the new coming with new virtues. Then, this valley, the humble heart, receives three things : it becomes more radiant and enlightened by grace, it becomes more ardent in charity, and it becomes more fruitful in perfect virtues and in good works. And thus you have the why, the way, and the work of this coming.

CHAPTER VII

OF THE BLESSED SACRAMENTS

THERE is still another coming of Christ our Bridegroom, taking place every day, with growth of grace and renewal of gifts. That is, when a man receives some sacrament with a humble heart void of anything contrary thereto. In this way he receives new gifts and more ample grace, because of his humility and through the mysterious working of Christ in the sacraments. Those things which are contrary to the sacraments are unbelief in Baptism, a lack of repentance in Confession, and approaching the Sacrament of the Altar in the state of mortal sin or with an evil intention ; and so on as regards the other sacraments. Those who act thus receive no new grace ; rather does their sinfulness increase.

This is the other coming of Christ our Bridegroom, which is present with us every day. We should consider it with a desiring heart, lest it should not take place within us ; for it is needful, if we are to remain steadfast and to go forward in eternal life.

CHAPTER VIII

OF THE THIRD COMING OF CHRIST

THE third coming, which is yet to be, will take place at the Judgment, or in the hour of death. The wherefore of this coming is the fitting time, the due cause, and the righteousness of the Judge.

The time which is fitting for this coming is the hour of death, and the Last Judgment of all men. When God created the soul out of nothing and united it with the body, He set a fixed day and a fixed hour known only of Him, when it should have to give up temporal things and to appear in His presence.

The due cause : for the soul must then account for every word spoken and for every deed done, before the Eternal Truth.

The righteousness of the Judge, for it is to Christ that this Judgment and this Verdict belong ; for He is the Son of Man and the Wisdom of the Father, and to this Wisdom all judgment is given, since all hearts, in heaven, and on earth, and in hell, are clear and open to It. And therefore these three points are the occasions of the general coming in the Day of Doom, and of the particular coming to each man in the hour of his death.

CHAPTER IX

SHOWING WHAT CHRIST WILL DO IN THE DAY OF DOOM

IN this Judgment Christ, our Bridegroom and our Judge, will reward and punish, according to justice ;

for He will give every man that which he has earned. He will give to the good, for every good work done in God, a wage without measure, that is to say, God's very Self, Whom no creature of itself can earn. But when God works these works with and through the creature, then by His power the creature gains His very Self as wage. And with due justice He will give eternal woe and eternal sorrow to the damned ; for these despised and rejected the Eternal Good for a good that cannot endure. And of their own free will they have turned away from God, and have set themselves against His glory and His will, and have sought after creatures ; and so shall they be justly condemned.

Those who bear witness at the Judgment are the angels and the conscience of men. And the adversary is the hellish fiend ; and the Judge is Christ, Whom none can deceive.

CHAPTER X

OF THE FIVE KINDS OF MEN WHO SHALL APPEAR AT THE JUDGMENT

FIVE kinds of men shall appear before this Judge.

The first, and the worst, are those Christians who have died in mortal sin, without repentance and without regret ; for these have despised the death of Christ and His sacraments, or else they have received them unworthily and in vain. And they have not practised the works of mercy, showing charity toward their neighbours, as God has commanded. And for this they are doomed to the depths of hell.

The second kind are the unbelievers, Pagans and Jews. These must all appear before Christ, though they were damned already during their lives; for, in their time, they possessed neither Divine grace nor Divine love, and for this reason they have always dwelt in the eternal death of damnation. But these shall have less pain than the evil Christians; for, since they received fewer gifts of God, they owed Him less loyalty.

The third kind are those good Christians who, from time to time, fell into sin, and rose again through contrition and penance; but who have not made full satisfaction for their sins according to justice. These belong to purgatory.

The fourth kind consists of those men who have kept God's commandments; or, when they broke them, they have returned to God with contrition and with penance, and with works of charity and mercy, and so have made satisfaction; so that their souls coming forth from their mouths go straight to heaven, without passing through purgatory.

The fifth kind are all those who, above all outward works of charity, have their sojourn in heaven, and are noughted and lost in God, and God in them, so that there is no other thing between God and them but time and their mortal nature. When these men are made free from their bodies, they enjoy, in that very moment, eternal bliss; and they are not judged, but shall themselves judge other men, with Christ, in the Day of Doom. And then all mortal life, and all temporal sorrows, both on earth and in purgatory, shall end, and all the souls of the damned, together with the Fiend and his companions, shall sink and disappear in the deeps of hell, in a corruption and everlasting horror without end. And in the twinkling of an eye the blessed shall be with Christ their Bridegroom in eternal glory ; and they shall see and taste and enjoy the fathomless riches of the Being of God, eternally and for ever.

This is the third coming, which all of us await, and which is still to happen. The first coming, when God became man and lived in humility among us, and died for the love of us, this coming we should imitate, outwardly by fulfilling the perfect moral virtues, inwardly by the practice of charity and true humility. In the second coming, which happens in the present time, He comes with grace within each loving heart ; and this coming we should long for and pray for every day, that we may remain steadfast and grow in new virtues. The third coming, at the Judgment, or in the hour of death, we should expect with longing, with trust, and with awe ; that we may be set free from this misery and enter into the house of glory.

This coming in its three ways is the second point of the four chief points, wherein Christ says : *Sponsus venit*, THE BRIDEGROOM COMETH.

CHAPTER XI

OF A SPIRITUAL GOING OUT WITH ALL VIRTUES

Now understand and mark this : Christ says, at the beginning of this precept, BEHOLD ; and this is done through charity and a pure conscience, as you have heard before. Then He has shown us what we shall see, that is, the threefold coming.

Now He commands us what we shall do next, and says : GO YE OUT. If you possess the first point, that is, if you are able to see, through grace and through charity ; and if, further, you have gazed well upon your pattern Christ and His going out ; then, there arises within you, out of charity, and out of the loving observation of your Bridegroom, a righteousness, namely, that thereafter you long to follow Him in the virtues. Then Christ is saying within you : GO YE OUT. This going out must be done in three ways : we must go out towards God, towards ourselves, and towards our neighbours, and this we must do by means of charity and righteousness. For charity ever strives towards the height, towards the kingdom of God, which is God Himself ; for He is the source from which unmediated charity flows forth, and wherein it abides in the Unity. And righteousness, which is born of charity, wills the perfection of all the moral and all the other virtues which are honourable and proper to the kingdom of God, that is the soul.

Charity and Righteousness : these two lay the foundation of the kingdom of the soul where God would dwell. And this foundation is humility.

These three virtues prop and bear the whole weight and the whole edifice of all the other virtues and of all transcendence. For charity always confronts man with the unfathomable goodness of God, from which it has flowed forth, that thereby he may live worthily and remain steadfast before God, and grow in true humility and all other virtues. And righteousness places man face to face with the eternal truth of God, that he may know truth, and become enlightened, and may fulfil all virtue without erring. But humility

brings man face to face with the most high mightiness
of God, that he may always remain little and lowly,
and may surrender himself to God, and may not stand
upon his selfhood. This is the way in which a man
should hold himself before God, that thereby he may
grow continually in new virtues.

CHAPTER XII

HOW HUMILITY IS THE FOUNDATION OF ALL OTHER VIRTUES

Now consider this : as we have laid down humility
as a foundation, so therefore we shall speak of humility
first.

Humility, that is lowliness or self-abasement, is
an inward bowing down or prostrating of the heart
and of the conscience before God's transcendent
worth. Righteousness demands and orders this, and
through charity a loving heart cannot leave it undone.
When a lowly and loving man considers that God
has served him so humbly, so lovingly, and so faithfully ; and sees God so high, and so mighty, and so
noble, and man so poor, and so little, and so low :
then there springs up within the humble heart a great
awe and a great veneration for God. For to pay
homage to God by every outward and inward act,
this is the first and dearest work of humility, the most
savoury among those of charity, and most meet
among those of righteousness. The loving and
humble heart cannot pay homage enough, either to
God or to His noble manhood, nor can it abase itself

as much as it would.   And that is why a humble man
thinks that his worship of God and his lowly service
are always falling short.   And he is meek, reverencing
Holy Church and the sacraments.   And he is discreet
in food and drink, in speech, in the answers which
he makes to everybody ;   and in his behaviour, dress,
and lowly service he is without hypocrisy and without pretence.   And he is humble in his devotions,
both outwardly and inwardly, before God and before
all men, so that none are offended because of him.
And so he overcomes and casts out Pride, which is
the source and origin of all other sins.   By humility
the snares of the devil, and of sin, and of the world,
are broken, and man is set in order, and established
in the very condition of virtue.   And heaven is
opened to him, and God stoops to hear his prayers,
and he is fulfilled with grace.   And Christ, that strong
rock, is his foundation.   Whosoever therefore grounds
his virtues in humility, he shall never err.

CHAPTER XIII

OF OBEDIENCE

FROM this humility there springs obedience, for none
can be inwardly obedient save the humble man.

Obedience means an unassuming, submissive, and
pliable humour, and a will in readiness for all that is
good.   Obedience makes a man submit to the biddings,
the forbiddings, and the will of God ; it subjects the
senses and the animal powers to the higher reason,
so that a man may live decently and reasonably.
And it makes men submissive and obedient to Holy

Church, to the sacraments, to the prelates and their teaching, to their commandments and their counsels, and to all the good customs practised by Holy Christendom. It also makes a man ready and supple in his intercourse with other men, in deed and counsel, in ghostly and bodily business, with prudent discretion, according to the needs of each.

And it casts out disobedience, that daughter of pride, more to be abhorred than venom or poison. To be obedient in will and deed adorns and enlarges and reveals the humility of a man. It makes peace in the cloister. If it is in the prelate, as it ought to be, it will draw to him all those whom he rules. It makes for peace and unanimity between equals; and he who has it is loved by his superiors and by those who are set over him; whilst by God he is advanced, and enriched with His gifts, which are eternal.

CHAPTER XIV

OF THE RENUNCIATION OF SELF-WILL

FROM this obedience there springs the renunciation of one's own will and one's own opinion, for none can submit his own will in all things to the will of another, save the obedient man: though one may obey in outward things and yet remain self-willed.

The forsaking of one's own will causes a man to live without preference for either this or that, in doing or leaving undone, in those things which are strange and special in the saints, in their precepts and in their practice; but it makes him to live always according to the glory and the commandments of God, and the will of his prelates, and in peace with all men in his neighbourhood, so far as true prudence permits.

By renouncing self-will in doing, in leaving undone, and in suffering, the material and occasion of pride are wholly cast out, and humility is made perfect in the highest degree. And God becomes the Lord of the man's whole will; and the man's will is so united with the will of God that he can neither will nor desire in any other way. This man has put off the old man, and has put on the new man, who is renewed and made according to the dearest will of God. Of all such Christ says : BLESSED ARE THE POOR IN SPIRIT —that is to say, those who have renounced self-will— FOR THEIRS IS THE KINGDOM OF HEAVEN.

CHAPTER XV

OF PATIENCE

FROM the renunciation of self-will springs patience ; for none can be perfectly patient in all things save the man who has subjected his own will to the will of God, and also in all profitable and seemly things, to the will of all other men.

Patience is a peaceful endurance of all things that may befall a man either from God or from the creatures. Nothing can trouble the patient man ; neither the loss of earthly goods, of friends and kinsmen ; nor sickness, nor disgrace, nor life, nor death, nor purgatory, nor devil, nor hell. For he has abandoned himself in perfect charity to the will of God, and as he is not burdened by mortal sin, everything that God imposes on him, in time and in eternity, is light to him. By this patience a man is also adorned and armed against peevishness and sudden wrath, and impatience in suffering ; which often stir a man from within and from without, and lay him open to many temptations.

CHAPTER XVI

OF MEEKNESS

FROM this patience there spring meekness and kindliness, for none can be meek in adversity save the patient man.

Meekness gives a man peace and rest in all things. For the meek man can bear provoking words and ways, uncivil looks and deeds, and every kind of injustice towards himself and his friends, and yet in all things remain in peace, for meekness is peaceful endurance.

By meekness the irascible or repulsive power remains unmoved, in quietude ; the desirous power is uplifted toward virtue ; the rational power, perceiving this, rejoices. And the conscience, tasting it, rests in peace ; for the second mortal sin, Anger, fury, or wrath, has been cast out. For the Spirit of God dwells in the humble and the meek ; and Christ says : BLESSED ARE THE MEEK, FOR THEY SHALL INHERIT THE EARTH, that is, their own nature and all earthly things, in meekness ; and after that the Country of Life in Eternity.

CHAPTER XVII

OF KINDLINESS

OUT of the same source wherein meekness takes its rise springs kindliness, for none can be kind save the meek man.

This kindness makes a man show a friendly face, and give a cordial response, and do compassionate deeds, to those who are quarrelsome, when he hopes that they will come to know themselves and mend their ways.

By gentleness and kindness, charity is kept quick and fruitful in man, for a heart full of kindness is like a lamp full of precious oil; for the oil of mercy enlightens the erring sinner with good example, and with words and works of comfort it anoints and heals those whose hearts are wounded or grieved or perplexed. And it is a fire and a light for those who dwell in the virtues, in the fire of charity; and neither jealousy nor envy can perturb it.

CHAPTER XVIII

OF COMPASSION

OUT of kindliness springs compassion, which is a fellow-feeling with all men; for none can share the griefs of all, save him who is kind.

Compassion is an inward movement of the heart, stirred by pity for the bodily and ghostly griefs of all men. This compassion makes a man suffer with Christ in His passion; for he who is compassionate

marks the wherefore of His pains and the way
of His resignation; of His love, His wounds, His
tenderness; of His grief and His nobleness; of the
disgrace, the misery, and the shame He endured; of
the way in which He was despised; of His crown;
of the nails; of His mercifulness; of His destruction
and dying in patience. These manifold and unheard-
of sorrows of Christ, our Saviour and our Bridegroom,
move all kindly men to pity and compassion with
Christ.

Compassion makes a man look into himself, and
recognize his faults, his feebleness in virtues and in
the worship of God, his lukewarmness, his laziness,
his many failings, the time he has wasted and his
present imperfection in moral and other virtues;
all this makes a man feel true pity and compassion
for himself. Further, compassion marks the errors
and disorders of our fellow-creatures, how little they
care for their God and their eternal blessedness, their
ingratitude for all the good things which God has
done for them, and the pains He suffered for their
sake; how they are strangers to virtue, unskilled
and unpractised in it, but skilful and cunning in every
wickedness; how attentive they are to the loss and
gain of earthly goods, how careless and reckless they
are of God, of eternal things, and their eternal bliss.
When he marks this, a good man is moved to compassion for the salvation of all men.

Such a man will also regard with pity the bodily
needs of his neighbours, and the manifold sufferings of human nature; seeing men hungry, thirsty,
cold, naked, sick, poor, and abject; the manifold
oppressions of the poor, the grief caused by loss of
kinsmen, friends, goods, honour, peace; all the

countless sorrows which befall the nature of man. These things move the just to compassion, so that they share the sorrows of all. But their greatest pain springs from this : that men are so impatient of this suffering, that they lose their reward, and may often earn hell for themselves. Such is the work of compassion and of pity.

This work of compassion and of common neighbourly love overcomes and casts out the third mortal sin, that is hatred or Envy. For compassion is a wound in the heart, whence flows a common love to all mankind and which cannot be healed so long as any suffering lives in man ; for God has ordained grief and sorrow of heart before all the virtues. And this is why Christ says : BLESSED ARE THEY THAT MOURN : FOR THEY SHALL BE COMFORTED. And that shall come to pass when they reap in joy that which now, through compassion and pity, they sow in tears.

CHAPTER XIX

OF GENEROSITY

FROM this compassion springs generosity ; for none can be generous in a supernatural way, with faithfulness and goodwill towards all, save him who has a pitiful heart—though a man may often show generosity to a particular person without charity and without supernatural generosity.

Generosity is a liberal flowing forth of the heart which has been touched by charity and pity. When a man considers with compassion the sufferings and the sorrows of Christ, therefrom springs generosity ;

which makes him offer to Christ, for His pains and for His love, praise and thanks, worship and adoration, with a joyful and humble surrender of body and soul, in time and in eternity. If a man considers himself with compassion, and has pity on himself, and thinks upon the good which God has done to him, and his own failings : then he must pour himself forth into the generosity of God, taking refuge in His faithfulness and His mercy, turning to Him with trust and with a perfect and free intention to serve Him for evermore. And the generous man who sees the errors and disorders of others, and their unrighteousness, beseeches and prays God, with ardent faith, that He will let His Divine gifts flow forth, that He will show His generosity to all men, and they may know Him and turn to the Truth. The generous man also marks with compassion the bodily needs of all men, and he serves, and he gives, and he lends, and he consoles everyone, according to the needs of each, in so far as he is able, with prudent discretion.

Because of this generosity men are wont to practise the seven works of mercy ; the rich do them by their alms and because of their riches, the poor by their good-will and by their hearty desire to do as the rich if they could. And thus the virtue of generosity is made perfect.

By generosity of heart all other virtues are increased, and all the powers of the soul are adorned ; for the generous man is always blithe in spirit and untroubled of heart, and he flows forth with desire, and in his works of virtue, to all men in common Whosoever is generous, and loves not earthly goods, how poor soever he be, he is like God : for all that he has in himself, and all that he feels, flow forth and are given away.   And in this way he has cast out the fourth mortal sin, which is covetousness or Avarice. Of all such Christ says : BLESSED ARE THE MERCIFUL, FOR THEY SHALL OBTAIN MERCY in that day when they shall hear these words : COME, YE BLESSED OF MY FATHER, INHERIT THE KINGDOM PREPARED FOR YOU— because of your mercy,—FROM THE FOUNDATION OF THE WORLD.

CHAPTER XX

OF ZEAL AND DILIGENCE

OUT of this generosity there spring a supernatural zeal and diligence in all virtues and all that is seemly. And none can feel this zeal save him who overflows with generosity.   It is an inward restless striving after every virtue, after the likeness of Christ and of all His saints.   In this zeal a man longs to devote his heart and his senses, his soul and his body, and all that he is, and all that he has and all toward which he aspires, to the glory and praise of God.

This zeal makes a man grow in reason and prudence, and practise the virtues, both of soul and of body, in righteousness.   Through this supernatural zeal all the powers of the soul are laid open to God, and are made ready for all virtues.   And the conscience rejoices, and the grace of God is increased ; the virtues are practised with joy and gladness, and the outward works are adorned.

Whosoever has received this living zeal from God has cast out the fifth mortal sin, which is indolence of the mind or Sloth, as regards the virtues which it is needful that we should practise.   And sometimes, this living zeal also casts out the sloth and indolence of the natural body.   Of all such Christ says: BLESSED ARE THEY WHICH DO HUNGER AND THIRST AFTER RIGHTEOUSNESS: FOR THEY SHALL BE FILLED, and this shall come to pass when the glory of God shall be manifest to them, and shall fill them, each according to his love and righteousness.

CHAPTER XXI

OF TEMPERANCE AND SOBRIETY

FROM this zeal there spring temperance and sobriety, both inward and outward; for none can possess the right measure of sobriety save him who is greatly zealous and diligent to keep his soul and body in righteousness. Sobriety divides the higher powers from the animal powers; it saves a man from intemperance and from excess. Sobriety wishes neither to taste, nor to know, those things which are forbidden.

The incomprehensible and most high Nature of God transcends all creatures in heaven and on earth. For all that a creature can comprehend is of the creature; but God is above all creatures and within and without all creatures, and every created comprehension is too narrow to comprehend Him. But if a creature is to comprehend and to understand God, it must be caught up beyond itself into God, and comprehend God with God. Whosoever then would know and understand what God is—which is not permitted—he would go mad. Behold, all

created light is powerless to know what God is.   What
God is in Himself, transcends all creatures ; but that
God exists, is testified by nature, and by Holy Writ,
and by every creature.   We should believe the articles
of faith, and not desire to understand them, for this
is impossible as long as we are here below : such is
sobriety. The mysterious and subtle teachings of
Holy Writ, inspired by the Holy Ghost, should not
be explained and understood in any other way than
in their bearing upon the lives of Christ and His
saints.   Man should consider nature, and the Scriptures, and all creatures, and take from these that
which profits him and nothing more.   Such is sobriety
of spirit.

A man should keep his senses in sobriety and should
restrain the animal powers by means of the reason ;
so that the lusts of the flesh do not enter too far into
the savouring of food and of drink ; but he should eat
and drink as the sick take their physic, because it
is needful to support his strength, that he may serve
God therewith.   This is sobriety of body.   He should
also observe method and moderation in doing and
in leaving undone, in words and in works, in silence
and in speaking, in food and in drink, according to
the custom of Holy Church, and after the example of
the saints.

By inward and ghostly temperance and sobriety a
man preserves firmness and constancy of faith, purity
of intelligence, that tranquillity of reason necessary
to the comprehension of truth, an impulse towards
all virtues according to the will of God, peace of
heart, and serenity of conscience.   And herewith he
possesses an enduring peace, in God and in himself.

And by temperance and sobriety of the outward

bodily senses, a man often preserves the health and the soundness of his natural body, the dignity of his outward life, and a good reputation. And thus he lives in peace with himself and with his neighbours; for by his temperance and sobriety he draws to himself and pleases all men of good-will. And thus he casts out the sixth mortal sin, which is intemperance, greed or Gluttony. Of all such Christ says: BLESSED ARE THE PEACEMAKERS: FOR THEY SHALL BE CALLED THE CHILDREN OF GOD; for they are like unto the Son, Who has made peace in every creature who desired peace. And whosoever makes peace in himself through his temperance and sobriety shall partake with Him of the inheritance of His Father; and shall possess it with Him in eternity.

CHAPTER XXII

OF PURITY

FROM this temperance there springs purity both of soul and of body, for none can be perfectly pure in body and in soul save him who is temperate in body and in soul.

Purity of spirit is this: that a man should not cleave to any creature with desirous affection, but to God alone; for we should use all creatures, but enjoy only God. Purity of spirit makes a man cleave to God, above all understanding, and above all feelings, and above all the gifts which God may pour into his soul: for all that a creature receives in his understanding and in his feeling, purity will pass by, to rest in God. Go therefore to the Sacrament of the Altar, not for the sake of refreshment, nor because of desire, nor for pleasure, nor for peace, nor for satisfaction, nor for sweetness, nor for anything else than the glory of God and your own growth in all virtues. This is purity of spirit.

Purity of heart is this : that a man, in every bodily temptation or natural inclination, of his own free will, and with an ever-renewed confidence and without hesitation, turns to God ; with an ever-renewed faithfulness and with a firm will ever to remain with Him. For consenting to those sins or satisfactions, which the bodily nature seeks like a beast, is a departure from God.

Purity of body is this : that a man withdraws from, and bewares of, all unchaste deeds, in whatsoever manner they be, which his conscience teaches and declares to be unchaste, and contrary to the commandments, the honour, and the will of God.

By these three kinds of purity the seventh mortal sin is overcome and cast out.; that is, Unchastity. And this is a consenting and turning of the spirit from God to some creaturely thing ; it is the unchaste work of the body contrary to the dispensation of Holy Church ; it is a sensual dwelling of the heart upon the taste or enjoyment of some creature, whatsoever it be. But thereby I do not mean those sudden movements of appetite and desire, which no one can prevent.

Now you should know that purity of spirit keeps a man in the likeness of God, untroubled by any creature, and inclined towards God, and united with Him.

Purity of body is likened to the whiteness of lilies and to the cleanness of the angels. In withstanding, it is likened to the redness of roses and to the nobleness of martyrs. If it is kept for the love and the glory of God, it is perfect. And so it is likened to the sunflower, for it is one of the highest ornaments of nature.

Purity of heart works a renewal and increase of the grace of God. By purity of heart all the virtues are prompted, practised and preserved. It guards and keeps the senses from without; it quells and restrains the animal lusts from within; it is an adornment of all inwardness. And it is the door of the heart; barred against all earthly things and all deceit, but opened to all heavenly things and to all truth. And of all such Christ says: BLESSED ARE THE PURE IN HEART: FOR THEY SHALL SEE GOD; and in this vision consist our eternal joy, our reward and our entrance into bliss. Therefore men should be sober and temperate in all things, and beware of all intercourse and occasion whereby purity, whether of soul or of body, may be defiled.

CHAPTER XXIII

OF THREE ENEMIES TO BE OVERCOME BY RIGHTEOUSNESS

Now, if we wish to possess these virtues, and to cast out their opposites, we must possess righteousness, and we must practise and preserve it in purity of heart unto death; for we have three powerful adversaries, who tempt us and make war on us at all times, in all places, and in many ways. If we make peace with one of these three, and become subject to him,

we are vanquished ; for the three of them agree
together in all iniquity.

These three adversaries are the devil, the world,
and our own flesh ; and this last is the nearest to us,
and often the worst and most harmful of all three
to us ; for our fleshly lusts are the weapons with
which our enemies make war on us. Idleness and indifference to virtue and the glory of God, these are
the causes and the occasions of the struggle. But the
weakness of our nature, our carelessness and ignorance
of truth, these are the swords with which our enemies
often wound, and sometimes conquer us.

And for this reason we should build up a wall and
make a separation within ourselves. And the lower
part of ourselves, which is beastly and contrary to
the virtues, and which wills our separation from God,
we should hate and persecute, and we should torment
it by means of penances and austerity of life ; so that
it be always repressed, and subject to reason, that
thereby righteousness and purity of heart may always
have the upper hand in all the works of virtue. And
all the suffering, grief, and persecution, which God
sends us through these enemies of virtue, we should
gladly bear for the glory of God, and for the honour
of the virtues, and that we may obtain and possess
righteousness in purity of heart ; for Christ says :
BLESSED ARE THEY WHICH ARE PERSECUTED FOR
RIGHTEOUSNESS' SAKE : FOR THEIRS IS THE KINGDOM
OF HEAVEN. For a righteousness which is maintained
in suffering and in virtuous deeds is like the penny
which is counted as heavy as the kingdom of God ;
and with it is bought eternal life.

And with these virtues a man goes out towards
God, towards himself, and towards his neigh-

bour, in good customs, in virtues, and in right-eousness.

CHAPTER XXIV

OF THE KINGDOM OF THE SOUL

WHOSOEVER wishes to obtain and to keep these virtues should adorn and possess and rule his soul like a kingdom. Free-will is the king of the soul. It is free by nature and still more free by grace. It shall be crowned with a crown that is called charity. The crown and the kingdom shall be received from the Emperor, Who is Lord and Master and King of kings ; and the kingdom should be possessed, ruled, and maintained in His name. This king, free-will, should dwell in the chief city of the kingdom ; namely, in the desirous power of the soul. And he should be clad and adorned with a garment of two parts. The right side of his garment should be a virtue called strength, that therewith he may be strong and mighty to overcome all hindrances, and to ascend up to heaven, into the palace of the most high Emperor, and to bow down his crowned head before the most high King, with love, and with self-surrendered desire. This is the proper work of charity : through it the crown is received, through it the crown is adorned, through it the kingdom is maintained and possessed in eternity. The left side of the garment should be a cardinal virtue called moral force. Through it, free-will, the king, shall quell all im-morality, and fulfil all virtues, and shall possess his kingdom in power, even unto death.

This king should also choose councillors in his

kingdom : the wisest in the country. These should
be two divine virtues : knowledge and discretion,
enlightened by the light of Divine grace. They
should dwell near the king, in a palace called the
rational power of the soul, and they should be clad
and adorned with a moral virtue called temperance,
so that the king may always do or leave undone
according to their counsels. By means of knowledge
our conscience shall be cleansed of all its failings and
adorned with all virtues ; and by help of discretion
we shall give and take, do and leave undone, be
silent and speak, fast and eat, listen and reply,.and
act in all things according to knowledge and discretion, clad in the moral virtue called temperance or
sobriety.

This king, free-will, should also appoint in his
kingdom a judge : that is, righteousness. This is a
divine virtue when it springs from love, and it is one
of the highest of moral virtues. This judge should
dwell in the heart, in the midst of the kingdom, in
the irascible power. And he should be adorned with
a moral virtue called prudence ; for righteousness
cannot be perfect without prudence. This judge,
righteousness, should travel through the kingdom
with the king's own power and majesty, and furnished
with the wisdom of the councillors, and with his own
prudence. And he should set up and cast down,
judge and condemn, kill and leave alive, put to the
torture, blind and restore sight, raise and suppress,
scourge and chastise, extirpate all vices, and order
all things according to righteousness.

The common people of the kingdom are all the
other powers of the soul, which should be grounded
in humility and godly fear, and should be subject

to God in all virtues, each power according to its own character.

Whosoever possesses, maintains, and has ordered, the kingdom of his soul in this way, has gone out with love and with virtue towards God, towards himself and towards his neighbour.

And this is the third of the four principal points which we would consider.

CHAPTER XXV

OF A SPIRITUAL MEETING OF GOD AND OURSELVES

WHEN a man through the grace of God is able to behold, and his conscience is clean, and he has considered the three comings of Christ our Bridegroom, and when he has gone out with the virtues : then there ensues the meeting with the Bridegroom, and that is the fourth point and the last. In this meeting lies all our bliss, the beginning and end of all virtue ; and without this meeting no virtue has ever been fulfilled.

Whosoever wishes to meet Christ as his beloved Bridegroom, and to possess in Him, and with Him, eternal life ; he must now, in time, go out to meet Christ at three points or in three ways. The first point is that he shall have God in mind in all things through which we earn eternal life. The second point is that there shall be nothing that he means or loves (4) more than God or even so much as God. And the third point is that he shall with great zeal seek to rest in God, above all creatures and above all God's gifts, above all the works of virtue and above all feelings that God may infuse into soul and body.

Now grasp this well : whosoever means God must
have God present in his mind under some godly
attribute ; and thereby he should mean only Him
Who is the Lord of heaven and earth and all creatures,
Who died for him, and Who can, and will, give him
eternal bliss.   In whatever way or under whatever
name we represent God to ourselves, if it be as the
Lord over all creatures, that is always right.   If we
conceive one of the Divine Persons, and in Him the
being and the might of the Divine Nature, that is
right.   If we set God before us as Maintainer, Re-
deemer, Creator, Ruler ; as Bliss, Power, Wisdom,
Truth, Goodness, and all this as within the abysmal
properties of the Divine Nature, that is right.

Though the names which we give to God are many,
the most high Nature of God is a Simplicity which
cannot be named by any creature.   But because of
His incomprehensible nobility and sublimity, which
we cannot rightly name nor wholly express, we give
Him all these names.   This is the way and the manner
of apprehension in which we should have God present
in our mind ; for, to mean God, this is to see God
in ghostly wise.   And to this intention charity and
love also belong ; for to know God and to be without
charity has no savour, neither does it help or further
us.   That is why a man should always in all his works
stretch towards God with love ; Whom, above all
things, he aims at and loves.   And this is going out
to meet God by intention and by love.

If a sinner would turn from his sins with full and
true repentance, he must go out to meet God in contrition and of his own free-will, and with an upright
purpose and intention to serve Him thenceforward
and never to sin any more.   Then, in this meeting,

he shall receive through the mercy of God a sure hope of eternal bliss and the remission of his sins ; and he shall further receive the foundation of all virtue : namely, Faith, Hope, and Charity, and a good-will toward all other virtues.

If this man wishes to go forward in the light of faith, and lay hold of all the works of Christ, and all His suffering ; all the things He promised us and did to us and will do to us until the Day of Doom and in eternity ; if that man wishes to lay hold of these that they may avail to his salvation : then he should go out to meet Christ once more, and should have Him ever in his sight, with praise and thankfulness and with a worthy acknowledgment of all His gifts, and all that He has done, and will do, in eternity. Then his faith will be strengthened ; and he will be more often, and more ardently impelled towards all virtues.

If, then, he wishes to go forward in the works of virtue, he must also go out to meet Christ with self-renunciation, neither seeking himself, nor pursuing things alien from God ; but let him be wise and discreet in all that he does, having in mind in all things God alone, and God's praise and glory, and let him continue therein even unto death. Thereby his reason is enlightened, and his charity is increased, and he grows in piety and in the aptitude for all virtues.

We should have God in mind in all our good works ; in evil works we cannot do this. We should not have in mind two ends ; that is to say; we should mean God alone and nothing else. All other ends should be subordinate to God, not opposed to God ; they should be, in their order, a help and a furtherance, that we may the better come to God.   And then we are in the right way.

We should also rather seek our rest upon Him and in Him Whom we mean and love, than in any of the messengers He sends ; that is to say, His gifts. The soul should also rest in God above all the jewels and all the gifts which it may send back to God by its own messengers.   The messengers of the soul are intention, love, and desire : these carry all good deeds and all virtues up to God.   But above all these things, above all multiplicity, the soul should rest in its Beloved.   In this way and in this wise we should go out to meet Christ with an upright inten- tion during all our lives, and in all our works, and in all our virtues ; so that we may also meet Him in the light of glory at the hour of death.

This method and this way, of which you have now heard, is called the Active Life.   It is needful for all men ; and these, at least, should not live contrary to virtue, even though they may not possess all the virtues in this perfection.   For, to live contrary to virtue is to live in sin ; for Christ says : HE THAT IS NOT WITH ME IS AGAINST ME.   Whosoever is not humble, he is proud ; and whosoever is proud and not humble does not belong to God.   And thus it is with all the sins and all the virtues ; either a man has the virtue and lives in grace, or else he has its opposite and lives in sin.   Let each man try himself, and live according to that which has here been shown.

CHAPTER XXVI

OF THE DESIRE TO KNOW THE BRIDEGROOM
IN HIS NATURE

A MAN who lives this life in its perfection, as it has here been shown, and who is offering up his whole life, and all his works, to the worship and praise of God, and who wills and loves God above all things, is often stirred by a desire to see, to know, and to prove what, in Himself, this Bridegroom Christ is; Who for man's sake became man and laboured in love unto death, and delivered us from sin and the devil, and has given us Himself and His grace, and left us His sacraments, and has promised us His kingdom and Himself as an eternal wage; Who also gives us all that is needful for the body, and inward consolation and sweetness, and innumerable gifts of all kinds, according to the needs of each.

When a man beholds all this, he feels an un-measured impulse to see Christ his Bridegroom, and to know Him as He is in Himself. Though he knows Him in His works, this does not seem to him enough. Then he must do as the publican Zaccheus did, who longed to see Jesus, who He was. He must run before the crowd, that is the multiplicity of creatures; for these make us so little and so low that we cannot see God. And he must climb up into the tree of faith, which grows from above downwards, for its roots are in the Godhead. This tree has twelve branches, which are the twelve articles of faith. The lower speak of the Divine Humanity, and of those things which belong to our salvation of soul and of body. The upper part of the tree tells of the Godhead, of the Trinity of Persons, and of the Unity of the Nature of God. And the man must cling to that unity, in the highest part of the tree; for there it is that Jesus must pass with all His gifts.

Here comes Jesus, and sees the man, and shows to him, in the light of faith, that He is according to His Godhead immeasurable and incomprehensible and inaccessible and abysmal, transcending every created light and every finite conception. And this is the highest knowledge of God which any man may have in the active life : that he should confess in the light of faith that God is incomprehensible and unknowable. And in this light Christ says to man's desire : MAKE HASTE AND COME DOWN, FOR TO-DAY I MUST ABIDE AT THY HOUSE. This hasty descent, to which he is summoned by God, is nothing else than a descent through desire and through love into the abyss of the Godhead, which no intelligence can reach in the created light. But where intelligence remains without, desire and love go in. When the soul is thus stretched towards God, by intention and by love, above everything that it can understand, then it rests and dwells in God, and God in it. When the soul climbs with desire above the multiplicity of creatures, and above the works of the senses, and above the light of nature, then it meets Christ in the light of faith, and becomes enlightened, and confesses that God is unknowable and incomprehensible. When it stretches itself with longing towards this incomprehensible God, then it meets Christ, and is filled with His gifts. And when it loves and rests above all gifts, and above itself, and above all creatures, then it dwells in God, and God dwells in it.

This is the way in which we shall meet Christ on

the summit of the active life. When you have laid the foundation of righteousness, charity, and humility ; and have established on it a dwelling-place, that is, those virtues which have been named heretofore ; and have met Christ through faith, by intention and by love ; then you dwell in God and God dwells in you, and you possess the true active life.

And this was the first of which we would speak.

THE END OF THE FIRST BOOK

HERE BEGINS
THE SECOND BOOK

PROLOGUE

THE wise virgin, that is the pure soul, having abandoned earthly things, and living according to the virtues for God, has taken in the vessel of her heart the oil of charity and of godly deeds, with the lamp of an unsullied conscience. But when Christ the Bridegroom tarries with His consolations, and the renewed inpouring of His gifts, the soul becomes drowsy, sleepy, and, inert. Then, at midnight, when it is least expected, a ghostly cry is made within the soul: BEHOLD, THE BRIDEGROOM, COMETH, GO YE OUT TO MEET HIM. Of this beholding, and of the inward coming of Christ, and of a man's ghostly going out, and of his meeting with Christ; of these four points we will now speak, and we will explain and apply them according to an inward, lofty, God-desiring life, which all cannot reach, but which many men attain through the moral virtues and inward zeal.

By these words Christ teaches us four things. First, that He wills that our understanding should be enlightened by supernatural light; this we learn from the word which He speaks: BEHOLD. Secondly, He shows us what we ought to see: namely, the inward coming of our Bridegroom, the Eternal Truth; this we understand from His saying: THE BRIDEGROOM

COMETH. Thirdly, He commands us to go out through inward exercises according to righteousness; for this reason He says: GO YE OUT. And, by the fourth point, He shows us the end and the aim of the whole; that is, the meeting with our Bridegroom Christ, in the fruitive unity of the Godhead.

CHAPTER I

HOW WE ACHIEVE SUPERNATURAL SIGHT IN OUR INWARD WORKINGS

Now concerning the first point. Christ says: BEHOLD. Whosoever wishes to see in a supernatural way in his inward exercises must have three things. The first is the light of Divine grace, and this in a more lofty degree than that which we can experience in the outward and active life without earnest inward diligence. The second thing is the casting out of all distracting images and attachments from the heart; so that the man may be free and imageless, released from all attachments, and empty of all creatures. The third thing is a free turning of the will, with a gathering together of all our powers, both bodily and ghostly, cleansed from every inordinate love. Thereby the will flows forth into the unity of God and into the unity of the mind; and thus the rational creature may obtain and possess the most high unity of God in a supernatural manner. For this God has created heaven and earth and everything; and for this reason He became man, and taught us, and lived for our sake, and has Himself become the Way to the unity. And He died in the bonds of love, and has ascended and has opened to us that very unity, in which we may possess eternal bliss.

CHAPTER II

OF A THREE-FOLD UNITY WHICH IS IN US BY NATURE

Now mark this with diligence : a threefold unity is found in all men by nature, and also in all good men according to a supernatural manner.

The first and highest unity of man is in God ; for all creatures depend upon this unity for their being, their life, and their preservation ; and if they be separated in this wise from God, they fall into the nothingness and become nought. This unity is in us essentially, by nature, whether we be good or evil. And without our own working it makes us neither holy nor blessed. This unity we possess within us and yet above us, as the ground and the preserver of our being and of our life.

The second unity or union is also in us by nature. It is the unity of our higher powers ; forasmuch as these spring naturally as active powers from the unity of the mind or of the spirit. This is that same unity which depends upon God ; but with this difference, that here it is active and there essential. Nevertheless, the spirit is wholly and perfectly understood according to the fulness of its substance, in each unity. This unity we possess within us, above our senses ; and from it there proceed memory, understanding, and will, and all the powers of ghostly action. In this unity, the soul is called " spirit."

The third unity which is in us by nature is the

source of all the bodily powers, in the unity of the heart; origin and beginning of the bodily life. This unity the soul possesses in the body and in the quickening centre of the heart, and therefrom flow forth all bodily activities, and the five senses. And therein the soul is called " soul " ; for it is the forming principle of the body, and quickens this carcase ; that is, gives it life and keeps it therein.

These three unities abide in man by nature as one life and one kingdom. In the lowest we are sensible and animal; in the middle we are rational and spiritual; and in the highest we are kept according to our essence. And thus are all men by nature.

Now these three unities, as one kingdom and one eternal dwelling-place, are adorned and inhabited in a supernatural way by the moral virtues through charity and the active life. And they are still more gloriously adorned and more excellently perfected by inward exercises united with a spiritual life. But they are most gloriously and blessedly adorned by a supernatural and contemplative life.

The lowest unity, being of the body, is supernaturally adorned and perfected through outward works and moral perfection, according to the way of Christ and His saints : and through bearing the cross with Christ, and through subordinating nature discreetly according to its powers to the commandments of Holy Church and to the doctrines of the saints.

The second unity, being in the spirit and wholly spiritual, is supernaturally adorned and perfected through the three divine virtues, Faith, Hope, and Charity; and through the inflow of the grace and the gifts of God; and through a good-will to follow the examples of Christ and Holy Christendom in all virtues.

The third and highest unity is above the comprehension of our reason, and yet essentially within us. We possess it in a supernatural way when in all our works of virtue we have in mind the praise and glory of God, and above all aims, above ourselves, and above all things would rest only in Him. This is that unity wherefrom we have come forth as creatures, and wherein, according to our being, we are at home. And by means of the virtues here named, these three unities are adorned in the active life.

Now we will show how these three unities are more highly adorned and more nobly fostered through an inward exercise joined to the active life. Whenever a man, because of his charity and his upright intention, lifts himself up with all his works and with his whole life toward the glory and the praise of God, ever seeking to rest in God above all things : then, in humble patience and self-surrender, yet with a sure trust, he will await new riches and new gifts ; but without anxiety as to whether it be God's good pleasure to give or not to give.

In this way one prepares and makes oneself ready to enter on the inward and God-desiring life. And, when the vessel is made ready, then the noble vintage is poured into it. And there is no vessel more noble than the loving soul, neither a vintage more wholesome than the grace of God. So a man should devote all his acts and all life to God, with a simple and upright intention directed to God ; and should rest, above intentions, and above himself, and above all things in that most high unity, in which God and the loving spirit are united without intermediary.

CHAPTER III

OF THE INFLOW OF THE GRACE OF GOD INTO OUR SPIRIT

FROM this unity, wherein the spirit is united with God without intermediary, grace and all gifts flow forth : and out of this same unity, where the spirit rests above itself in God, Christ the Eternal Truth says : BEHOLD, THE BRIDEGROOM COMETH, GO YE OUT TO MEET HIM. Christ, who is the light of Eternal Truth, says : BEHOLD : for through Him we become seeing ; for He is the light of the Father, and without Him there were no light, neither in heaven nor on earth. This speaking of Christ within us is nothing else than an inrush of His light and His grace. This grace pours into us in the unity of our higher powers and of our spirit ; wherefrom, through the power of the grace received, the higher powers flow out to become active in all virtues, and whereto, because of the bond of love, they ever return again.

In this unity lie the power for, and beginning and end of, every natural and supernatural work of the creature in so far as it is wrought in a creaturely way, through grace and Divine gifts, and by the creature's own strength. And therefore God pours His grace into the unity of the higher powers, that therewith man may always fulfil the virtues, through the power and the richness and the thrust of grace. For God gives us grace, therewith to work ; and above all graces He gives Himself, for fruition and for rest. The unity of our spirit is our dwelling-place, in the peace of God and in the riches of charity ; and there all the manifold virtues are gathered together, and live in the simplicity of the spirit.

Now the grace of God, pouring forth from God, is an inward thrust and urge of the Holy Ghost, driving forth our spirit from within and exciting it towards all virtues. This grace flows from within, and not from without ; for God is more inward to us than we are to ourselves, and His inward thrust or working within us, be it natural or supernatural, is nearer to us and more intimate to us, than our own working is. And therefore God works in us from within outwards ; but all creatures work from without inwards. And thus it is that grace, and all the gifts of God, and the Voice of God, come from within, in the unity of our spirit ; and not from without, into the imagination, by means of sensible images.

CHAPTER IV

SHOWING HOW WE SHOULD FOUND OUR INWARD LIFE ON A FREEDOM FROM IMAGES

Now Christ says in ghostly wise in the man who is turned within : BEHOLD. Three things, as I have said, make a man seeing in his inward exercise. The first is a shining forth of the grace of God. The grace of God in a soul is like a candle in a lantern or in a glass vessel ; for it enlightens, and brightens, and shines through, the vessel, that is, the righteous man. And it manifests itself to the man who has it within him, if he be observant of himself. And it manifests itself through him, to other men, in virtues and in good example. This flash of divine grace inwardly stirs and moves a man with swiftness, and this swift movement is the first thing which makes us see.

Of this swift movement of God there springs from the side of man the second thing, which is a gathering together of all inward and outward powers in the unity of the spirit, in the bonds of love. The third point is the freedom which allows the man to turn inwards, without hindrance from sensible images, as often as he wills and thinks upon his God. This means that a man must be indifferent to gladness and grief, profit and loss, rising and falling, to strange cares, to delight and to dread, and never be attached to any creature. These three things make a man seeing in his inward exercise. If you have these three, you have the foundation and the beginning of the inward practice and the inward life.

CHAPTER V

OF A THREE-FOLD COMING OF OUR LORD IN THE INWARD MAN

Even though the eye be clear and the sight keen, if there were no loveworthy and desirable object, clearness of sight would neither please nor profit a man. And this is why Christ shows to the enlightened eyes of the understanding what they shall see, to wit, the inward coming of Christ their Bridegroom.

Three ways of this special inward coming of God are found in those men who exercise themselves with devotion in the inward life ; and each of these three comings raises a man to a higher degree and to a more inward exercise.

The first coming of Christ in inward working drives and urges a man in his inward feeling ; it draws him with all his powers upwards to heaven, and it calls him to unite himself with God.   This driving and drawing we feel in the heart, and in the unity of all the bodily powers, and especially in the desirous power.   For this coming stirs, and works in, the lower part of man ; for this must be wholly purged and adorned, and inflamed and drawn inwards.   This inward urge of God gives and takes, makes rich and poor, brings weal and woe upon a man ; it causes hope and despair ; it burns and it freezes.   But no tongue can tell of those gifts and works and contraries that here come to pass.

This coming with its working is parted into four degrees, each one higher than the other, as we will show afterwards.   And with it the. lower part of man is adorned in the inward life.

CHAPTER VI

OF THE SECOND COMING OF OUR LORD IN THE INWARD MAN

THE second way in which Christ comes inwardly, with a higher nobleness, more after His likeness, with increased gifts, and with a greater radiance, is a pouring forth of the riches of His Divine gifts into the higher powers of the soul, whereby the spirit is strengthened, enlightened, and enriched in many ways. This streaming of God into us demands of us a flowing out and a flowing back, with all these riches, into that same Source from which that torrent has flowed. And in this torrent God gives to us and shows to us great wonders ; but He asks back from the soul all

His gifts, increased beyond anything that any creature could accomplish. This exercise and this way is more noble and more like unto God than the first ; and by it the three higher powers of the soul are adorned.

CHAPTER VII

OF THE THIRD COMING OF OUR LORD

THE third way in which our Lord comes inwardly is by an inward stirring or touch in the unity of the spirit, wherein are the higher powers of the soul ; wherefrom they flow forth, and to which they return again, and with which they always remain united in the bonds of love and through the natural unity of the spirit. In this coming consists the highest and most interior condition of the inward life ; and by it the unity of the spirit is adorned in many ways.

Now, in each coming, Christ desires of us a special going out of ourselves, toward a life that shall accord with the way of His coming. And therefore He says in ghostly wise within our hearts at each coming : GO YE OUT in your lives and in your practices in the way in which My graces and My gifts shall urge you. For according to the manner and way in which the Spirit of God urges, and drives, and draws, and streams into us, and stirs us ; in this way we must go out and progress in our inward practices, if we are to become perfect. But if we withstand the Spirit of God by a life that does not accord with it, we lose that inward urge, and then the virtues will depart from us.

These are the three comings of Christ, in inward

exercises. We will now explain and set forth each coming separately. Attend therefore with diligence; for he who never has himself felt or experienced this, he shall not easily understand it.

CHAPTER VIII

HOW THE FIRST COMING HAS FOUR DEGREES

THE first coming of Christ in the exercise of desire is, as we have said, an inward and sensible thrust of the Holy Ghost, urging and driving us towards all virtues. This coming may be likened to the splendour and the power of the sun, which, from the moment when it rises, enlightens and brightens and warms the whole world.   So likewise Christ, the eternal Sun, beams and shines, dwelling above the summit of the spirit; and enlightens and enkindles the lowest part of man, namely, the fleshly heart and the sensible powers. And this happens in a moment of time, shorter than the twinkling of an eye; for God's work is swift. But that man in whom this should take place must be inwardly seeing, with the eyes of the understanding.

In the higher lands, in the middle region of the world, the sun shines upon the mountains, bringing an early summer there, with good fruits and strong wine, and filling that land with joy. The same sun gives its splendour to the lower lands, at the utmost part of the earth. There the country is colder, and the power of the heat less; nevertheless, there too it produces many good fruits, though little wine. The men who dwell in the lower parts of themselves, in their outward senses, yet with a good intention, in moral virtues, in outward work, and in the grace of God : they too produce the good fruits of virtue, in great numbers and in many ways ; but of the wine of inward joy and ghostly consolation they taste little.

Now the man who wishes to feel within himself the glow of the Eternal Sun, which is Christ Himself, he should be seeing, and should dwell on the mountains in the higher lands, by a gathering together of all his powers, and lifting up his heart towards God, free and careless of joy and grief, and of all created things. There Christ, the Sun of righteousness, shines upon the free and uplifted heart : and these are the mountains that I mean.

Christ, the glorious Sun, the Divine Brightness, by His inward coming and by the power of His Spirit, enlightens and brightens and enkindles the free heart and all the powers of the soul. And this is the first work of the inward coming in the exercise of desire. Like as the power and the nature of fire enkindles everything which is offered to the flames, so Christ, by the fiery ardour of His inward coming, enkindles every ready, free and uplifted heart ; and in this coming He says : GO YE OUT by exercises according to the way of this coming.

CHAPTER IX

OF UNITY OF HEART

OF this ardour there springs unity of heart ; for we cannot achieve true unity unless the Spirit of God blows to a flame His fire in our hearts. For this fire makes one with itself and like to itself all that it can master and re-shape.

Unity is this: that a man feel himself to be gathered together with all his powers in the unity of his heart. Unity brings inward peace and restfulness of heart. Unity of heart is a bond which draws together body and soul, heart and senses, and all the outward and inward powers and encloses them in the union of love.

CHAPTER X

OF INWARDNESS

FROM this unity springs inwardness; for none can be inward save him who is gathered together in unity within himself. Inwardness means that a man is turned within, into his own heart, that thereby he may understand and feel the interior workings, and the interior words of God. Inwardness is a sensible fire of love, which the Spirit of God has blown to a flame, and which urges a man from within; and he knows not whence it comes nor what has befallen him.

CHAPTER XI

OF SENSIBLE LOVE

FROM inwardness there springs a sensible love, which fulfills the man's heart and the desirous power of the soul. This yearning love, and this sensible fruition of the heart, none can have save he who is inward of heart.

Sensible love is a yearning and savouring delight which we feel in God as the eternal Good, wherein are all other goods. Sensible love forsakes all creatures as regards pleasure, not as regards need. Inward love feels itself moved from within by the Eternal Love ; and this it must ever cherish. Inward love easily foregoes and despises all things that it may obtain that which it loves.

CHAPTER XII

OF DEVOTION

OF this sensible love is born devotion to God and to His glory. For none can have within his heart the hunger of devotion save him who bears within himself a sensible love of God. Where the fire of love sends up the flames of its desire to heaven, there is devotion. Devotion moves and draws a man, both from without and from within, towards the service of God. Devotion makes body and soul to blossom in nobility and worth before God and before all men. Devotion is demanded of us by God in every service which we ought to do to Him. Devotion purifies the body and the soul of everything that can stop and hinder us. Devotion shows and bestows the right way at blessedness.

CHAPTER XIII

OF GRATITUDE

INWARD devotion often brings forth gratitude; for none can thank and praise God so well as the inward and devout man. And it is just that we should thank and praise God, because He has created us as reasonable creatures, and has ordained and destined heaven and earth and the angels to our service; and because He became man for our sins, and taught us, and lived for our sake, and showed us the way; and because He has ministered to us in humble raiment, and suffered an ignominious death for the love of us, and promised us His eternal kingdom and Himself also for our reward and for our wage. And He has spared us in our sins, and has forgiven us or will forgive us; and has poured His grace and His love into our souls, and will dwell and remain with us, and in us, throughout eternity. And He has visited us and will visit us all the days of our lives with His noble sacraments, according to the need of each, and has left us His Flesh and His Blood for food and drink, according to the desire and the hunger of each; and has set before us nature and the Scriptures and all creatures, as examples, and as a mirror, that therein we may look and learn how we may turn all our deeds to works of virtue; and has given us health and strength and power, and sometimes for our own good has sent us sickness; and in outward need has established inward peace and happiness in us; and has caused us to be called by Christian names and to have been born of Christian parents. For all these things we should thank God here on earth, that hereafter we may thank Him in eternity.

We should also praise God by means of everything that we can offer to Him. To praise God, means that all his life long a man glorifies, reverences and venerates the Divine Omnipotence. The praise of God is the meet and proper work of the angels and the saints in heaven, and of loving men on earth. God should be praised by desire, by the lifting up of all our powers, by words, by works, with body and with soul, and with whatsoever one possesses; in humble service, from without and from within. He who does not praise God while here on earth shall in eternity be dumb. To praise God is the dearest and most joyous work of every loving heart; and the heart which is full of praise desires that every creature should praise God. The praise of God has no end, for it is our bliss; and most justly shall we praise Him in eternity.

CHAPTER XIV

OF TWO GRIEFS WHICH ARISE FROM INWARD GRATITUDE

FROM inward gratitude and praise there arises a two-fold grief of the heart and torment of desire. The first grief is, that we feel ourselves to lag behind in thanking, praising, glorifying and serving God. The second is, that we do not grow in charity, in virtue, in faith, and in perfect behaviour as much as we desire, that we may become worthy to thank and praise and serve God as it is proper to do.

This is the second grief. These two are root and fruit, beginning and end, of all inward virtues.

Inward grief and pain for our shortcomings in virtue and the praise of God, is the highest effect of this first degree of the inward exercise; and by it this degree is perfectly achieved.

CHAPTER XV

A SIMILITUDE HOW WE SHOULD PERFORM THE FIRST DEGREE OF OUR INWARD EXERCISE

Now consider in a similitude, how this inward exercise should be performed. When the natural fire has by its heat and power stirred water, or some other liquid, until it bubbles up; then this is its highest achievement. Then the water boils up and falls down to the bottom, and is then stirred again to the same activity by the power of the fire: so that the water is incessantly bubbling up, and the fire incessantly stirring it.

And so likewise works the inward fire of the Holy Ghost. It stirs and goads and drives the heart and all the powers of the soul until they boil; that is, until they thank and praise God in the way of which I have told you. And then one falls down to that very ground, where the Spirit of God is burning. So that the fire of love ever burns, and the man's heart ever thanks and praises God with words and with works and yet always abides in lowliness; esteeming that which he should do and would do to be great, and that which he is able to do to be small.

CHAPTER XVI

ANOTHER SIMILITUDE CONCERNING THE SAME EXERCISE

WHEN summer draws near and the sun rises higher, it draws the moisture out of the earth through the roots, and through the trunks of the trees, into the twigs ; and hence come foliage, flower, and fruit.

So likewise, when Christ the Eternal Sun rises and ascends in our hearts, so that it is summer in the adornment of our virtues, He gives His light and His heat to our desires, and draws the heart from all the multiplicity of earthly things, and brings about unity and inwardness ; and makes the heart grow and bring forth the leaves of inward love, the flowers of ardent devotion, and the fruits of thanksgiving and praise, and makes these fruits to endure eternally, in humble grief, because of our shortcomings.

Here ends the first of the four chief degrees of that inward working whereby the lowest part of man is adorned.

CHAPTER XVII

OF THE SECOND DEGREE OF OUR INWARD EXERCISE, WHICH INCREASES INWARDNESS BY HUMILITY

BUT, having likened the four degrees of the first coming of Christ to the splendour and the power of the sun, we also find in the sun another power and another action, which hastens the ripening, and increases the numbers, of the fruit.

When the sun rises very high, and enters the sign of *Gemini* (that is, the Twins ; or a twofold thing of one nature), which happens in the middle of the month of May : then it has a double power over flowers and herbs and everything that grows out of the earth. If, then, the planets which govern nature are well ordered according to the need of the season, the sun shines upon the earth and draws the moisture into the air. Thence come dew and rain ; and the fruits increase and multiply.

So likewise, when Christ that bright Sun has risen in our hearts above all things; when the demands of our bodily nature which are opposed to the spirit have been curbed and discreetly set in order ; when we have achieved the virtues in the way of which you have heard in the first degree ; when, lastly, through the ardour of our charity, all the pleasure, and all the peace, which we experience in these virtues, have been offered up and devoted to God, with thanksgiving and praise :—then, of all this there may come down a sweet rain of new inward consolation and the heavenly dew of the sweetness of God. This makes the virtues grow, and multiplies them twofold if we hinder it not. This is a new and special working, and a new coming, of Christ into the loving heart. And by it a man is lifted up into a higher state than that in which he was before. On this height Christ says : Go ye out according to the way of this coming.

CHAPTER XVIII

OF THE PURE DELIGHT OF THE HEART AND THE SENSIBLE POWERS

FROM this sweetness there springs a well-being of the heart and of all the bodily powers, so that a man thinks himself to be inwardly enfolded in the divine embrace of love. This delight and this consolation are greater and more pleasant to the soul and the body than all the satisfactions of the earth, even though one man should enjoy them all together. In this well-being God sinks into the heart by means of His gifts; with so much savoury solace and joy that the heart overflows from within. This makes a man comprehend the misery of those who live outside love. This well-being melts the heart to such a degree, that the man cannot contain himself through the fulness of inward joy.

CHAPTER XIX

OF SPIRITUAL INEBRIATION

FROM this rapturous delight springs spiritual inebriation. Spiritual inebriation is this; that a man receives more sensible joy and sweetness than his heart can either contain or desire. Spiritual inebriation brings forth many strange gestures in men. It makes some sing and praise God because of their fulness of joy, and some weep with great tears because of their sweetness of heart. It makes one restless in all his limbs, so that he must run and jump and dance; and so excites another that he must gesticulate and clap his hands. Another cries out with a loud voice, and so shows forth the plenitude he feels within; another must be silent and melt away, because of the rapture which he feels in all his senses. At times he thinks that all the world must feel what he feels: at times he thinks that none can taste what he has attained. Often he thinks that he never could, nor ever shall, lose this well-being ; at times he wonders why all men do not become God-desiring. At one time he thinks that God is for him alone, or for none other so much as for him ; at another time he asks himself with amazement of what nature these delights can be, and whence they come, and what has happened to him. This is the most rapturous life (as regards our bodily feelings) which man may attain upon earth. Sometimes the excess of joy becomes so great that the man thinks that his heart must break. And for all these manifold gifts and miraculous works, he shall, with a humble heart, thank and praise and honour and reverence the Lord, Who can do all this ; and thank Him with fervent devotion because it is His will to do all this. And the man shall always keep in his heart and speak through his mouth with sincere intention : " Lord, I am not worthy of this ; yet I have need of Thy boundless goodness and of Thy support." In such humility he may grow and rise into higher virtues.

CHAPTER XX

WHAT MAY HINDER A MAN IN THIS INEBRIATION

WHEN, however, this coming and this degree are granted to such men as first begin to turn from the world ; even though their conversion be perfect, and they have abandoned all worldly consolation, that they may be wholly God's, and may live altogether for Him,—yet they are still feeble and have need of milk and sweet things, and not of the strong food of fierce temptation and the loss of God. And in this season, that is to say, in this state, hoar-frost and fog often harm such men ; for it is just in the middle of May according to the course of the inward life. Hoar-frost is the desire to be somewhat or the belief that one is somewhat ; or to be attached to one's self, or to suppose that we have earned these consolations and are worthy of them. This is hoar-frost, which may destroy the flowers and fruits of all the virtues. Fog is, the desire to rest in inward consolations and sweetness. This darkens the air of the reason ; and the powers, which ought to open and flower, close again. And thereby one loses the knowledge of truth, and yet may keep a certain false sweetness, which is given by the devil, and which in the end shall lead us astray.

CHAPTER XXI

A SIMILITUDE HOW A MAN SHOULD ACT AND BEAR HIMSELF IN THIS CASE

Now I will give you a short similitude, that you may not err in this case, but may govern yourselves prudently. You should watch the wise bee and do as it does. It dwells in unity, in the congregation of its fellows, and goes forth, not in the storm, but in calm and still weather, in the sunshine, towards all those flowers in which sweetness may be found. It does not rest on any flower, neither on any beauty nor on any sweetness ; but it draws from them honey and wax, that is to say, sweetness and light-giving matter, and brings both to the unity of

the hive, that therewith it may produce fruits, and
be greatly profitable.

Christ, the Eternal Sun, shining into the open heart,
causes that heart to grow and to bloom, and it overflows with all the inward powers with joy and sweetness.

So the wise man will do like the bee, and he will fly
forth with attention and with reason and with discretion, towards all those gifts and towards all that
sweetness which he has ever experienced, and towards
all the good which God has ever done to him.   And in
the light of love and with inward observation, he will
taste of the multitude of consolations and good things ;
and will not rest upon any flower of the gifts of God,
but, laden with gratitude and praise, will fly back
into the unity, wherein he wishes to rest and to dwell
eternally with God.

This is the second degree of that inward working
which adorns the lower part of man in many ways.

CHAPTER XXII

OF THE THIRD DEGREE OF THE SPIRITUAL COMING
OF CHRIST

WHEN the sun has risen in the heavens as high as it
can, it stands in the sign of *Cancer* (which means
Crab, because it cannot go further, but begins to go
back).   Then come the fiercest heats of the whole
year.   And the sun draws up all the moisture, and the
earth becomes dry, and the fruits ripen quickly.

So likewise, when Christ, the Divine Sun, has risen
to the zenith of our hearts—that is, above all the
gifts and consolations and sweetness which we may

receive from Him—so that we do not rest in any savours, how great soever they be, which God may pour into our souls; if then, masters of ourselves, we ever turn inwards, by the way which has been shown heretofore, with humble praise and with fervent thanksgiving, towards the very source from which all gifts flow forth according to the needs and the merits of each creature : then Christ stands on high in the zenith of our hearts, and He will draw all things, that is, all our powers, to Himself. When thus neither savour nor consolation can overcome or hinder the loving heart, but it would rather forgo all consolations and all gifts, that it may find Him Whom it loves : then there arises from this the third kind of inward exercise, by which man is uplifted and adorned in his sensibility and the lower part of his being.

The first work of Christ, and the beginning of this degree consists in this : that God draws the heart, the desires, and all the powers of the soul up towards heaven, and calls them to be united with Him, and says in ghostly wise within the heart : Go YE OUT of yourselves by the way in which I draw and invite you. This drawing and this inviting I cannot well make plain to gross and insensitive men ; but it is an inward constraining and drawing of the heart towards the most high unity of God. This inward summons is joyful to the loving heart above anything it ever experienced before. For hence arise a new way and a higher exercise.

Here the heart opens itself in joy and in desire, and all the veins gape, and all the powers of the soul are in readiness, and desire to fulfil that which is demanded of them by God and by His unity. This invitation is a shining forth of Christ, the Eternal Sun ; and

it brings forth such great pleasure and joy in the
heart, and makes the heart open so widely, that it
can never wholly close again.   And thereby a man
is wounded in the heart from within, and feels the
wound of love.   To be wounded by love is the sweetest
feeling and the sharpest pain which any one may endure.
To be wounded by love is to know for certain that one
shall be healed ; for the ghostly wound brings woes
and weal at the same time.   For Christ, the true Sun
streams and shines into the wounded and open heart
and calls it to oneness again.   And this renews the
wound and all its pangs.

CHAPTER XXIII

OF THE PAIN AND RESTLESSNESS OF LOVE

OF this inward demand and this invitation, and also
because the creature lifts itself up and offers itself,
and all that it can do, and yet can neither attain nor
acquire the unity—of these things spring a ghostly
pain.   When the inmost part of the heart and the
source of life have been wounded by love, and
one cannot obtain that which one desires above all
things, but must ever abide where one does not
wish to be :   from these two things pain comes forth.
Here Christ is risen to the zenith of the conscience,
and He sends His Divine rays into the hungry desires
and into the longings of the heart ; and this splendour
burns and dries up and consumes all the moisture,
that is, the strength and the powers of nature.   The
desire of the open heart, and the shining of the Divine
rays, cause a perpetual pain.

If, then, one cannot achieve God and yet cannot and will not do without Him, from these two things there arise in such men tumult and restlessness, both without and within. And so long as a man is thus agitated, no creature, neither in heaven nor on earth, can give him rest or help him. In this state there are sometimes spoken from within sublime and salutary words, and singular teachings and wisdom are given. In this inward tumult one is ready to suffer all that can be suffered, that one may obtain that which one loves. This fury of love is an inward impatience which will hardly use reason or follow it, if it cannot obtain that which it loves. This inward fury eats a man's heart and drinks his blood. Here the sensible heat of love is fiercer than at any other stage in man's whole life ; and his bodily nature is secretly wounded and consumed without any outward work, and the fruits of the virtues ripen more quickly than in all the degrees which have been shown heretofore.

In the like season of the year, the visible sun enters the sign of *Leo*, that is, the Lion, who is fierce by nature, for he is the lord over all beasts. So likewise, when a man comes to this way, Christ, the bright Sun, stands in the sign of the Lion, for the rays of His heat are so fierce that the blood in the heart of the impatient man must boil. And when this fierce way prevails, it masters and subdues all other ways and works ; for it wills to be wayless, that is, without manner. And in this tumult a man sometimes falls into a desire and restless longing to be freed from the prison of his body, so that he may at once be united with Him Whom he loves. And he opens his inward eyes and beholds the heavenly house full of glory and joy, and his Beloved crowned in the midst of it, flowing forth towards His saints in abounding bliss; whilst he must lack all this. And therefrom there often spring in such a man outward tears and great longings. He looks down and considers the place of exile in which he has been imprisoned, and from which he cannot escape; then tears of sadness and misery gush forth. These natural tears soothe and refresh the man's heart, and they are wholesome to the bodily nature, preserving its strength and powers and sustaining him through this state of tumult. All the manifold considerations and exercises according to ways or manner are helpful to the impatient man; that his strength may be preserved and that he may long endure in virtue.

CHAPTER XXIV

OF ECSTACIES AND DIVINE REVELATIONS

By this fierce ardour and this impatience some men are at times caught into the spirit, above the senses; and there words are spoken to them and images and similitudes shown to them, teaching them some truth of which they or other men have need, or else things that are to come. These are called revelations or visions. If they are bodily images, they are received in the imagination. This may be the work of an angel in man, through the power of God. If it be an intellectual truth, or a ghostly image, through which God reveals Himself in His unfathomableness, this is received in the understanding; and the man can clothe it in words in so far as it can be expressed in words. Sometimes a man may also be drawn above himself and above the spirit (but not altogether outside himself) into an Incomprehensible Good, which he shall never be able either to utter or to explain in the way in which he heard and saw ; for in this simple act and this simple vision, to hear and to see are one. And none can work this in man, without intermediary and without the co-operation of any creature, save God alone. It is called RAPTUS ; which means, rapt away, or uplifted, or carried away. At times God grants to such men a sudden spiritual glimpse, like the lightning in the sky. It comes like a sudden glimpse of strange brightness, shining forth from the Simple Nudity. And thereby for an instant the spirit is raised above itself ; but the light passes at once and the man returns to himself again. This is the work of God Himself ; it is something very sublime ; for those to whom it happens often become illuminated men.

Other things sometimes happen to those who live in the fierce ardour of love ; for often another light shines into them, and this is the work of God through means. In this light the heart and the desirous powers uplift themselves towards that light ; and, in the meeting with that light, the joy and the satisfaction are so great that the heart cannot contain them, but breaks out in a loud voice with cries of joy. And this is called the JUBILUS, or jubilation ; that is, a joy which cannot be uttered in words. And one cannot contain oneself ; but if one would go out with an opened and uplifted heart to meet this light the voice must follow, so long as this exercise and this light endure. Some inward men are at times taught in a dream by their guardian angels or by other angels, concerning many things of which they have need. Some men too are found who have many sudden intuitions, or inspirations, or imaginations, and also have miraculous dreams, and yet remain in their outward senses. But these know nothing of the tumult of love ; for they dwell in outward multiplicity, and love has not wounded them. These things may be natural, or they may come from the devil, or from good angels, and therefore we may have faith in them so far as they accord with Holy Writ, and with the truth, but no more. If we trust them beyond this, we may easily be deceived.

CHAPTER XXV

AN EXAMPLE SHOWING HOW ONE IS HINDERED IN THIS EXERCISE

Now I will show you the hindrances and the dangers which he meets with who dwells in the fury of love. In this time, as you have heard, the sun is in the sign of the Lion ; and this is the most unhealthy period of the year, although it is fruitful ; for here begin the dog-days, which bring many a plague with them. Then the weather may become so unwholesome and so hot that in some countries herbs and trees wither and shrivel, and in some waters the fishes pine away and perish, and on the land men also sicken and die. And this is not caused only by the sun, for then it would be the same everywhere ; in all countries and in all waters, and with all men. But the cause of it is often the corruption and the disorder of the matter on which the sun's power works. So likewise it is when a man comes into this state of impatience. He enters in truth into the dog-days, and the splendour of the Divine rays burns so fiercely and so hotly from above, and the heart wounded by love is so inflamed from within—since the ardour of affection and the impatience of desire have been thus enkindled—that the man falls into impatience and striving, even as a woman who labours in child-birth and cannot be delivered. If the man then look steadfastly into his own wounded heart, and at Him Whom he loves, these woes grow without ceasing. So greatly does the torment increase that the man withers and shrivels in his bodily nature, even as the trees in hot countries; and he dies in the fury of love, and enters the kingdom of heaven without passing through purgatory. But though he dies well who dies of love, as long as a tree may bear good fruit, it should neither be felled nor uprooted. Sometimes God flows forth with great sweetness into the turbulent heart. Then the heart swims in bliss, as a fish in water ; and the inmost ground of the heart burns in the fury of love, even whilst it swims in delight in the gifts of God, because of the blissful and impatient ardour of the loving heart itself. And to dwell long in this degree consumes the bodily nature. All men who burn in the fury of love must pine away in that state ; but those who can govern themselves well do not die.

CHAPTER XXVI

ANOTHER EXAMPLE

AND now I will warn you against another thing which may cause great harm. Sometimes in that hot season there falls the honey-dew of a certain false sweetness, which pollutes the fruit, or utterly spoils it. And it is most apt to fall at noon, in bright sunshine, and in big drops; and it is hardly to be distinguished from rain. So likewise, some men may be robbed of their outward senses by a certain light produced by the devil. And in this light they are enwrapped and ensnared, and at the same time many kinds of images, both false and true, are shown to them, and they are spoken to in diverse ways; and all this is seen and received of them with great delight. And here there fall sometimes the honey-drops of a false sweetness, in which a man may find his pleasure. He who esteems it much receives much of it : and thereby the man is easily polluted, for if he will hold for true those things which are not like to truth, for the reason that they have been shown or spoken to him, he falls into error and the fruit of virtue is lost. But those who have trodden the ways whereof I have written before, though they may be tempted by this spirit and this light, they will recognise them and will not be harmed.

CHAPTER XXVII

A PARABLE OF THE ANT

A BRIEF parable I will give to those who dwell in the tumult of love, that they may endure this state nobly and becomingly, and may attain to higher virtues. There is a small insect called the ant. It is strong and sagacious, and very loth to die. It lives by choice amongst the congregation of its fellows, in hot and dry soil. The ant works during summer, and gathers grain for food for the winter. And it splits the grain

in two lest it should sprout and be spoiled, and be of
no use when nothing can be gathered anymore. And
it seeks no strange ways, but always goes forth by
the same way. And if it abides its time, it shall be
able to fly.

Thus should these men do. They should be strong
in abiding the coming of Christ, sagacious against the
communications and inspirations of the devil. They
should not desire death; but God's glory alone, and
for themselves new virtues. They should dwell in
the congregation of their heart and of their powers,
and should follow the drawing and the inviting of
the Divine Unity. They should dwell in warm and
dry soil, that is, in the fierce tumult of love and in
a great restlessness. And they should labour during
the summer of this life, and gather the fruits of virtue
for eternity; and they should split these fruits in
two. The one part is, that they should ever desire
the most high fruition of Eternity; and the other
part is that, by means of the reason, they should
always restrain themselves as much as they can, and
abide the time which God has ordained to them, and
thus the fruit of virtue is preserved unto eternity.
And they should not follow strange paths or singular
ways; but they should follow the track of love
through all storms to that place whither love shall
lead them. And if they abide the time, and persevere
in all virtues, they shall behold the Mystery of God
and take flight towards It.

CHAPTER XXVIII

OF THE FOURTH DEGREE OF THE COMING OF CHRIST

Now we will speak further of the fourth manner of the coming of Christ, uplifting and perfecting a man by inward exercise in the lower part of his being. But having likened all the inward comings to the splendour of the sun, and to its power, according to the course of the year, we will speak further, according to the course of the seasons, of another action and another work of the sun.

When the sun first begins to descend from the zenith to the nadir, it enters the sign which is called *Virgo*, that is, the Virgin, because now the season becomes unfruitful, as a virgin is. (In this time the glorious Virgin Mary, the mother of Christ, ascended to heaven, full of joy and rich in all virtues.) At this time the heat begins to grow less; and men begin to gather in, for use during the rest of the year, those ripe and lasting fruits which can be kept and consumed long afterwards, such as corn and wine and the durable fruits, which have now come to their maturity. And a part of the same corn is sown, so that it be multiplied for the benefit of men. In this season all the work of the sun of the whole year is perfected and fulfilled.

So likewise, when Christ the glorious Sun has risen to the zenith in a man's heart, as I have taught you in the third degree; and when He then begins to descend and to hide the shining of His Divine rays, and to forsake the man; then the heat and impatience of love begin to grow less. Now when Christ thus hides Himself, and withdraws the shining of

His brightness and His heat, this is the first work, and the new coming, of this degree. Then Christ speaks in ghostly wise within this man, saying : " GO YE OUT in such wise as I will now show you." So the man goes out, and finds himself poor and miserable and forsaken. Here all the tempest and fury and impatience of love grow less, and the hot summer passes into autumn, and all its riches are turned to great poverty. Then the man begins to complain because of his wretchedness : Whither has gone the ardent love, the inwardness, the gratitude, the joyful praise ? And the inward consolation, the intimate joy, the sensible savour, how has he lost them ? How have the fierce tempest of love, and all the other gifts which he felt before, become dead in him ? And he feels like an ignorant man who has lost all his pains and his labour. And often his natural life is troubled by such a loss.

Sometimes these unhappy men are also deprived of their earthly goods, of friends, of kinsmen ; and they are abandoned of all creatures, their holiness is not known or esteemed, men speak evil of their works and their whole lives, and they are despised and rejected by all their neighbours. And at times they fall into sickness and many a plague, and some into bodily temptations ; or, that which is worst of all, into temptations of the spirit.

From this poverty arise a fear lest one should fall, and a kind of half-doubt. This is the utmost point at which a man can hold his ground without falling into despair. Such a man likes to seek out good men, and to complain to them, and show them his miseries ; and he desires the help and prayers of Holy Church and of all the just.

CHAPTER XXIX

SHOWING WHAT THE FORSAKEN MAN SHOULD DO

HERE the man should bethink himself with a humble heart that of his own he has nothing but misery; and he should say in resignation and self-abandonment the words which were spoken by the holy man Job : " THE LORD GAVE, AND THE LORD HATH TAKEN AWAY ; as it pleased the Lord, so it hath been done ; BLESSED BE THE NAME OF THE LORD." And he should renounce himself in all things, and should say and mean in his heart, " Lord, I am as willing to be poor in all those things of which I have been deprived as I am ready to be rich, O Lord, if it be Thy will and to Thy glory ; not my will according to nature, O Lord, but Thy will and my will according to spirit be done. For I am Thine own, O Lord, and would as well be in hell as in heaven, if it were to Thy glory. Lord, do unto me according to Thy good pleasure." Of all this suffering and abandonment the man should make an inward joy ; and he should give himself into the hands of God, and should be glad because he is able to suffer for the glory of God. And if he be true to this disposition, he shall taste such an inward joy as he never tasted before ; for nothing is more joyful to the lover of God, than to feel that he belongs wholly to his Beloved. And if he has indeed followed the way of the virtues straight to this degree, even though he has not passed through all the states which have been pointed out heretofore, it is not needful, if he feels within himself the source of the virtues : which is in activity, humble obedience ; and, in passivity, patient resignation. In these two things this degree is established in everlasting surety.

In this season of the year the sun of heaven enters the sign of *Libra*, which means the Scales; for day and night are evenly balanced, and the sun divides the light from the darkness in equal parts. So likewise Christ stands in the sign of the Balance for the resigned man. Whether He gives sweetness or bitterness, darkness or light, whatever he lays upon the scale, the man balances it evenly; all things are equal to him, save sin alone, which is for ever cast out. When such utterly resigned men have thus been deprived of all consolation, and believe that they have lost all virtues, and are forsaken of God and of all creatures: then if they are able to reap them, all kinds of fruit, the corn and vine, are ready and ripe. And this image means, that all that the body can endure, whatsoever it be, should be offered up to God gladly, and of one's own free will, and without resistance to the supreme Will. All the outward and inward virtues, which a man practised with joy in the fire of love; these, since he knows them and is able to perform them, he should now practise diligently and with courage, and should offer them up to God. Never were they so dear to God; for never were they so noble and so fair. All the consolations which God ever gave should gladly be given up, if it be to His glory. This is the harvest of the corn, and of all kinds of ripe fruits, on which we shall live eternally, and which make us rich in God. Thus the virtues are made perfect, and sorrow is turned to eternal wine. By such men, and by their lives and their patience, all those who know them and all their neighbours are taught and changed for the better : and so the corn of their virtues is sown and multiplied for the benefit of all good men.

This is the fourth way in which a man by inward working is adorned and perfected in the bodily powers and the lower part of himself : and in no other way can he continually grow and become more perfect. But as such men have been harshly afflicted, and have been tried, and tempted, and combatted, by God, by their own selves, and by all creatures, in them the virtue of resignation reaches a singular perfection. Nevertheless, resignation, or the renunciation of self-will for the will of God, is before all things needful for all men who wish to be saved.

CHAPTER XXX

A PARABLE : HOW ONE MAY BE HINDERED IN THIS FOURTH DEGREE

AT this season of the year, so soon as the equinox is come, the sun begins to descend and the weather becomes cooler. And then some imprudent men become full of noxious humours, which enter into the stomach, and spoil the health and bring many diseases : and these destroy the appetite and the taste of good food, and bring many to death. And some men are corrupted by these noxious humours, so that they get dropsy, and have therefrom long torments and sometimes die. And from the superabundance of these humours come sickness and fever, from which many men suffer, and of which some die. And so likewise it is, when men of good-will, who once tasted God, have swerved from Him and from truth, and have gone astray ; these either sicken in the way of perfection, or wither away as regards virtue, or fall into eternal death, through one of these maladies, and some through all three. Especially when he is forsaken a man has need of much strength, and must exercise himself in the way I have just taught you : thus he shall not be deceived. But the unwise man, who rules himself ill, falls easily into these maladies ; for in him the weather has grown cooler. For this reason his nature becomes slow in virtue and in good works, and craves for comfort and softness of the body ; often without discretion and more than is needful. And other men would like well to receive solace from God, if they might partake of Him without pains and labour. And some seek for solace in creatures, where-from great harm often ensues. And some think themselves sick and feeble and that their powers are exhausted, and believe that they have need of all that they can get, and that they must cherish their bodies in comfort and repose. When a man yields himself in such a way, and seeks without discretion after bodily things and comforts ; then all such things are noxious humours which fulfil the stomach, that is to say, the man's heart, and take from him the taste and the enjoyment of good food, that is to say, of all the virtues.

CHAPTER XXXI

OF ANOTHER HINDRANCE

IF a man thus falls into sickness and cold, he is some-times caught by dropsy, that is to say, he has an inclination towards the outward possession of earthly

things. The more such men acquire, the more they
desire ; for they straightway become dropsical. The
belly, that is, the appetites or lusts, swells terribly,
and the thirst will not be quenched. But the face of
conscience and discretion becomes small and thin,
for these men put hindrances against the inflow of
the grace of God. If they thus accumulate the waters
of earthly possessions about the heart, that is, if they
cling to them with desire, they cannot progress in
works of charity ; for they are sick, they lack the
inward spirit of life and breath, that is to say, they
lack the grace of God and inward charity. And
therefore they cannot rid themselves of the waters
of earthly riches : the heart is submerged in them,
and they are often choked therein and die an eternal
death. But those who keep the waters of earthly
riches far below the heart, so that they are master
of their possessions and can renounce them whenever
it is needful : these, though they may suffer long
from inordinate inclinations, may yet be cured.

CHAPTER XXXII

OF FOUR KINDS OF FEVER WHEREWITH A MAN MAY BE TORMENTED

THOSE men who are full of noxious humours, that is
to say, full of inordinate inclination towards bodily
comfort and towards foreign and creaturely consolations, can fall into four kinds of fever.

The first kind is called the quotidian fever. It is
a multiplicity of the heart , for these men wish to
know all things, and to speak of all things, and to
criticise and to judge all things, and meanwhile they

often fail to observe themselves. They are weighed down by many strange cares; they must often hear what they do not like; and the least thing troubles them. Their thoughts are restless; first this, then that, first here, then there; they are like to the winds. This is a daily fever; for they are troubled, and busied, and in multiplicity, from morning until evening, and sometimes in the night also, whether they sleep or wake. Though this may exist in a state of grace and without mortal sin, yet it hinders inwardness and inward practices and takes away the taste of God and of all virtues. And this is an eternal loss.

The second kind of fever comes on alternate days. It is called fickleness. If it lasts long it is often dangerous. This fever is of two kinds: sometimes it comes from intemperate heat, and sometimes from cold. The one which comes from intemperate heat befalls certain good men; for when they are, or have been, touched by God, and then are forsaken of Him, they sometimes fall into fickleness. To-day they choose one way of life, and to-morrow another; at one time they wish to be silent, and another time they wish continually to speak. First they wish to enter into this order, then into that. First they wish to give all their goods to God, then they wish to keep them. At one time they wish to wander abroad, at another to be enclosed in a cell. At one time they long to go often to the Sacrament, and shortly afterwards they value this but little. At one time they wish to pray much in a loud voice, and another time but shortly after, they would keep silence. And this is both a vain curiosity and a fickleness, which hinder and impede a man from comprehending inward truth, and destroy in him both the source and the practice of all inwardness. Now mark whence this unstable condition comes in some good men. When a man sets his thoughts and his inward active endeavour on the virtues and on outward behaviour more than on God and on union with God : though he remains in the grace of God (for in the virtues he aims at God), yet none the less his life is unstable, for he does not feel himself to rest in God above all virtues. And therefore he possesses something that he does not know ; for, Him Whom he seeks in the virtues and in the multiplicity of acts, he possesses within himself, above intention, above virtues, and above all ways and means. And therefore, if this man would overcome his fickleness, he must learn to rest above all virtues in God and in the most high Unity of God.

The other fever of fickleness, which comes from cold, all those men have who love God indeed, but at the same time seek and inordinately love some other thing. This fever comes from cold ; for the heat of charity is poor indeed where not God alone, but foreign things besides and with God, urge and excite us towards the works of virtue. Such men are fickle of heart ; for in all the things which they do, nature is secretly seeking its own, often without their knowledge, for they know not themselves. Such men choose and abandon, first one way of life, then another. To-day they choose one priest, to whom they would go for confession and for counsel their whole life long ; and to-morrow they will choose another. On all things they will ask advice, but hardly ever do they act upon it. All things for which they are blamed and rebuked they like to excuse and to justify. Of fine words they have plenty, but little is in them. They like well to have a reputation for virtue, but without great effort. They wish their virtues to be known, and these are therefore empty, and have no savour either of God nor of themselves. Others they teach, but will themselves hardly be taught or reproved. A natural self-love and a hidden pride make them thus fickle. Such people walk on the verge of hell : one false step, and into it they fall.

In some men this fever of fickleness may produce the quartan fever ; that is, an estrangement from God and from themselves and from truth and from all virtues. And then they fall into such confusion that they are at their wit's end and know not what to do. This illness is more dangerous than either of the others.

Through this estrangement a man sometimes falls into a fever which is called the double quartan, which means indifference. Then the fourth day is doubled, and he can hardly recover, for he becomes indifferent and heedless of all that is needful to eternal life. So he may fall into sin, like one who never knew anything of God. If this may befall those men who govern themselves ill in this state of abandonment, then it behoves those to beware who never knew ought of God, nor of the inward life, nor of that sweet savour which good men find in their exercises.

CHAPTER XXXIII

SHOWING HOW THESE FOUR DEGREES IN THEIR PERFECTION ARE FOUND IN CHRIST

IF we wish to progress rightly in the four aforesaid degrees of the inward exercise which adorn a man's bodily powers and the lower part of his nature, we should mark Christ, Who taught us these four ways and has gone before us therein. Christ, the bright Sun, rose in the heavens of the most high Trinity, and in the dawn of His glorious mother, the Virgin Mary; who was, and is, the dawn and daybreak of all those graces in which we shall rejoice eternally.

Now mark this: Christ had, and still has, the first degree; for he was one and in oneness. In Him were, and are, gathered and united all the virtues that ever were, and ever shall be, practised; moreover all the creatures who ever practised, and ever shall practise, these virtues. Thus He was the Father's Only Begotten Son, and was united with human nature. And He was inward; for He brought to earth the fire that inflamed all the saints and all good men. And He yielded a sensible love and loyalty to His Father, and to all those who shall enjoy Him in eternity. And His devotion and His loving and aspiring heart burned and groaned before His Father because of the miseries of all men. His whole life, and all His works, from without and from within, and all His words, were thanksgiving and praise, and glorifying of His Father. This is the first degree.

Christ, the Sun of Love, sparkled and shone brighter still, and more ardently; for in Him was, and is, the fulness of all graces and gifts. And for this reason the heart of Christ and His way of life, and His conduct, and His service, over-flowed in mercy, in gentleness, in humility, and in generosity ; and He was so gracious and so lovable that His ways and His person drew all men of goodwill. He was the unspotted lily amidst the flowers of the field, wherefrom all the just may suck the honey of eternal sweetness and eternal consolation. For all the gifts which were ever bestowed upon the manhood of Christ, Christ thanked and praised, according to His manhood, His Eternal Father, Who is the Father of all gifts ; and He rested, as regards the highest powers of His soul, above all gifts, in the most high Unity of God, from which all gifts flow forth. Thus He possessed the second degree.

Christ the glorious Sun sparkled and shone higher still, and brighter, and more ardently ; for all the days of His life long His bodily powers and His senses, His heart and His mind, were called and destined of His Father to that most high glory and beatitude which He now enjoys, according to His senses and His bodily powers. And He Himself was both naturally and supernaturally inclined thereto, according to His affections ; nevertheless He was willing to abide in this exile until the time that His Father had foreseen and ordained from eternity. Thus He possessed the third degree.

When the due time had come wherein Christ should reap, and carry into the Eternal Kingdom, the fruits of all those virtues which ever had ripened, or ever should ripen, then the Eternal Sun began to descend ; for then Christ humbled Himself, and delivered His bodily life into the hands of His enemies. And in this distress He was denied and forsaken of

His friends, and from His human nature there was withdrawn all inward and outward consolation ; and there was laid on it misery and sorrow, buffettings, blasphemies, and heavy burdens, and it paid the price of all our sins according to justice.   And He bore these things in humble patience, and, whilst He was thus forsaken, He wrought the greatest work of love.   And, thereby He has bought back and redeemed our eternal heritage.   Thus is He adorned in the lower part of His noble manhood ; for in it He suffered these pains for our sins.   And this is why He is called the Saviour of the world, and why He is glorified, honoured, and exalted, and set on the right hand of His Father, where He reigns in mightiness ; and all creatures, in heaven, and on earth, and in hell, bow the knee eternally before His most high Name.

CHAPTER XXXIV

SHOWING HOW A MAN SHOULD LIVE IF HE WOULD BE ENLIGHTENED

THE man who lives in true obedience and in the moral virtues, according to the commandments of God, and besides this practises the inward virtues according to the teaching and stirring of the Holy Ghost ; who is just in deed and in word, who seeks not his own, neither in time nor in eternity, who can bear with equanimity and with true patience, darkness and heaviness, and all kinds of miseries, and thanks God for everything, and offers himself up with humble resignation : he has received the first coming of Christ according to the way of inward exercise.   And he has gone out from himself in the inward life, and has adorned with rich virtues and gifts his quickened heart and the unity of his body and senses. When such a man has been altogether purified and set at rest, and is gathered together into unity as regards his lower powers, he can be inwardly enlightened, if God deems that the time is fit and he craves it. It may also come to pass, that a man may be enlightened at the beginning of his conversion, if he yield himself wholly to the will of God and renounce all selfhood ; all lies in this. Such a man, however, must afterwards pass through those degrees and ways of the outward and the inward life which have been shown heretofore ; but this would be easier to him than to another, who mounts from below upwards, for he has more light than the other man.

CHAPTER XXXV

OF THE SECOND COMING OF CHRIST, OR, THE FOUNTAIN WITH THREE RILLS

Now we will speak further of the second manner of the coming of Christ, in those inward exercises by which a man is adorned, enlightened, and enriched in the three highest powers of the soul. This coming we will liken to a living fountain with three rills.

The fountain-head, from which the rills flow forth, is the fulness of Divine grace within the unity of our spirit. There grace dwells essentially ; abiding as a brimming fountain, and actively flowing forth in rills into all the powers of the soul, each according to its need. These rills are special inflowings or workings of God in the higher powers, wherein God works by means of grace in many diverse ways.

CHAPTER XXXVI

THE FIRST RILL ADORNS THE MEMORY [1]

THE first rill of grace, which God causes to flow forth in this coming, is a pure simplicity, shining in the spirit without differentiation. This rill takes its rise from the fountain within the unity of the spirit; and it flows straight downwards and pours through all the powers of the soul, the lower and the higher; and raises them above all multiplicity and all busyness and produces simplicity in a man; and shows and gives him the inward bond of unity of spirit. Thus he is lifted up as regards his memory, and is freed from distracting images and from fickleness.

Now in this light, Christ demands a going out in conformity with this light and with this coming. So the man goes out, and knows and finds himself, through this simple light which has been poured into him, to be united and established and penetrated and confirmed, in the unity of his spirit or mind. Thereby the man is raised up and set in a new state, and he turns inwards, and fixes his memory upon the Nudity, above all the distractions of sensible images, and above multiplicity. Here the man possesses the essential and supernatural unity of his spirit, as his own dwelling-place and as his own eternal, personal heritage. He ever has a natural and a supernatural tendency towards this same unity; and this same unity through the gifts of God and through simplicity of intention, shall have an eternal loving tendency

---

[1] It should be remembered that for the mediæval psychologist the term " memory " included all that we mean by "mind."

towards that most high Unity, where, in the bond of the Holy Ghost, the Father and the Son are united with all saints. And thus the first rill, which demands unity, is satisfied.

CHAPTER XXXVII

THE SECOND RILL ENLIGHTENS THE UNDER-STANDING

THROUGH inward charity and loving inclination and the faithfulness of God, there arises the second rill from the fulness of grace within the unity of the spirit; and it is a ghostly light which flows forth and shines into the understanding, discerning diverse things. For this light shows and proves in truth the distinctions between all the virtues; but this does not lie wholly in our power. For, even if we always had this light within our souls, it is God Who makes it to be silent and to speak, and He may show it and hide it, give it and take it away, in any time and place; for this light is His. And He therefore works in this light when He wills, and where He wills, and for whom He wills, and what He wills. These men have no need of revelations, neither of being caught up above the senses; for their life, and dwelling-place, their way, and their being, are in the spirit, above the senses and above sensibility. And there God shows to such men what is His good pleasure, and what is needful for them or for other men. Nevertheless God could, were such His will, deprive such men of their outward senses, and show them from within unknown similitudes and future things in many ways.

Now Christ wills that this man go out and walk in this light, in the way of this light. Therefore this enlightened man shall go out and shall mark his state and his life from within and from without, and see whether he is perfectly like unto Christ, according to His manhood and according to His Godhead. For we have been created in the image and after the likeness of God. And he shall raise his enlightened eyes, by means of the illuminated reason, to the intelligible Truth, and mark and behold in a creaturely way the most high Nature of God and the fathomless attributes which are in God: for to a fathomless Nature belong fathomless virtues and activities.

The most high Nature of the Godhead may thus be perceived and beheld: how it is Simplicity and One-foldness, inaccessible Height and bottomless Depth, incomprehensible Breadth and eternal Length, a dark Silence, a wild Desert, the Rest of all saints in the Unity, and a common Fruition of Himself and of all saints in Eternity. And many other marvels may be seen in the abysmal Sea of the Godhead; and though, because of the grossness of the senses to which they must be shown from without, we must use sensible images, yet, in truth, these things are perceived and beheld from within, as an abysmal and unconditioned Good. But if they must be shown from without, it must be done by means of diverse similitudes and images, according to the enlightenment of the reason of him who shapes and shows them.

The enlightened man shall also mark and behold the attributes of the Father in the Godhead: how He is omnipotent Power and Might, Creator, Mover, Preserver, Beginning and End, the Origin and Being of all creatures. This the rill of grace shows to the enlightened reason in its radiance. It also shows the attributes of the Eternal Word : abysmal Wisdom and Truth, Pattern of all creatures and all life, Eternal and unchanging Rule, Seeing all things and Seeing Through all things, none of which is hidden from Him ; Transillumination and Enlightenment of all saints in heaven and on earth, according to the merits of each. And even as this rill of radiance shows the distinctions between many things, so it also shows to the enlightened reason the attributes of the Holy Ghost : incomprehensible Love and Generosity, Compassion and Mercy, infinite Faithfulness and Benevolence, inconceivable Greatness, outpouring Richness, a limitless Goodness drenching through all heavenly spirits with delight, a Flame of Fire which burns all things together in the Unity, a flowing Fountain, rich in all savours, according to the desire of each ; the Preparation of all saints for their eternal bliss and their entrance therein, an Embrace and Penetration of the Father, the Son, and all saints in fruitive Unity. All this is observed and beheld without differentiation or division in the simple Nature of the Godhead. And according to our perception these attributes abide as Persons do, in manifold distinctions. For between might and goodness, between generosity and truth, there are, according to our perception, great differences. Nevertheless all these are found in oneness and undifferentiation in the most high Nature of the Godhead. But the relations which make the personal attributes remain in eternal distinction. For the Father begets distinction. For the Father incessantly begets his Son, and Himself is unbegotten ; and the Son is begotten, and cannot beget ; and thus throughout eternity the Father has

a Son, and the Son a Father. And these are the
relations of the Father to the Son, and of the Son to
the Father. And the Father and the Son breathe
forth one Spirit, Who is Their common Will or Love.
And this Spirit begets not, nor is He begotten ; but
must eternally pour forth, being breathed forth from
both the Father and the Son. And these three
Persons are one God and one Spirit. And all the
attributes with the works which flow forth from them
are common to all the Persons, for They work by virtue
of Their Onefold Nature.

.   .   .   .   .   .

The incomprehensible richness and loftiness of the
Divine Nature, its outpouring generosity toward all
in common, fills a man with wonder. And, above
all, he wonders at the universality of God and His
outpouring upon all things.· For he beholds the incomprehensible Essence as a common fruition of
God and all saints. And he sees the Divine Persons
as a common outpouring and a common activity in
grace and in glory, in nature and above nature, in
all places and at all times, in saints and in men, in
heaven and on earth, in all creatures, rational,
irrational, and material, according to the merits, the
need, and the receptivity of each. And he beholds
heaven and earth, sun and moon, the four elements,
together with all creatures, and the course of the
heavens, created for all in common. God, with all
His gifts, is common to all : the angels are common :
the soul is common to all its powers, to the whole
body, to all its members, yet in each member is
entire ; for the soul cannot be divided, save by the
reason. For though, according to the reason, the
highest powers and the lowest, the spirit and the soul,

are certainly divided; yet, in nature, they are one. So too God is whole and special to each, and yet common to all creation; for by Him all things are; within Him and upon Him, heaven and earth and all nature depend. When a man thus considers the wonderful wealth and loftiness of the Divine Nature, and all the multiplicity of gifts which He gives and offers to His creatures, then there grows up within him a wonder at such manifold richness, at such loftiness, and at the immeasurable faithfulness of God to His creatures. And thence springs a particular inward gladness of the spirit, and a high trust in God, and this inward gladness envelops and drenches all the powers of the soul and the most inward part of the spirit.

CHAPTER XXXVIII

THE THIRD RILL ESTABLISHES THE WILL TO EVERY PERFECTION

FROM this gladness and the fulness of grace and the faithfulness of God, there is born and flows forth the third rill in this same unity of the spirit. This rill, like a fire, enkindles the will, and swallows up and consumes everything into unity. And it fills to the brim and flows through all the powers of the soul, with rich gifts and with a singular nobility: and it calls forth in the will a tender spiritual love without effort.

Now Christ says inwardly within the spirit by means of this burning brook: GO YE OUT by practices in conformity with these gifts and with this coming.

By the first rill, which is a simple light, the memory
has been lifted above sensible images, and has been
grounded and established in the unity of the spirit.
By the second rill, which is an inflowing light, understanding and reason have been enlightened, to know
the diverse ways of virtue and of practice, and discern the mysteries of the Scriptures. By the third
rill, which is an inpouring heat, the supreme will has
been enkindled in tranquil love, and has been endowed with great riches. Thus has this man become
spiritually enlightened; for the grace of God dwells
like a fountainhead in the unity of his spirit; and
its rills cause in the powers an outflowing with all
the virtues. And the fountainhead of grace ever
demands a flowing-back into the same source from
whence the flood proceeds.

CHAPTER XXXIX

SHOWING HOW THE ESTABLISHED MAN SHALL GO OUT IN FOUR WAYS

Now the man who is established in the bonds of love
shall dwell in the unity of the spirit; and he shall
go out with enlightened reason and with overflowing
love in heaven and on earth; and he shall mark all
things with clear discernment; and he shall dispense
and distribute all things, out of true generosity, and
because of his richness in God.

In four ways this enlightened man is invited and
urged to go out. The first going out shall be towards
God and towards all saints; the second going out
shall be towards sinners and towards all perverted

men ; the third going out shall be towards purgatory ; and the fourth, towards himself and towards all good men.

CHAPTER XL

HE SHALL GO OUT TOWARDS GOD AND TOWARDS ALL SAINTS

Now understand this : this man shall go out and observe God in His glory with all saints. And he shall behold the rich and generous outflowing of God, with glory, and with Himself, and with inconceivable delights towards all the saints, according to the longing of all spirits ; and how these flow back, with themselves, and with all that they have received and can achieve, towards that same rich Oneness from which all bliss comes forth.

This flowing forth of God always demands a flowing back ; for God is a Sea that ebbs and flows, pouring without ceasing into all His beloved according to the need and the merits of each, and ebbing back again with all those who have been thus endowed both in heaven and on earth, with all that they have and all that they can. And of some He demands more than they are able to bring, for He shows Himself so rich and so generous and so boundlessly good : and in showing Himself thus He demands love and adoration according to His worth. For God wishes to be loved by us according to the measure of His nobility, and in this all spirits fail ; and therefore their love becomes wayless and without manner, for they know not how they may fulfil it, nor how they may come to it. For the love of all spirits is measured : and for this reason their love perpetually begins anew, so that God may be loved according to His demand and to the spirits' own desires. And this is why all blessed spirits perpetually gather themselves together and form a burning flame of love, that they may fulfil this work, and that God may be loved according to His nobility. Reason shows clearly that to creatures this is impossible; but love always wills the fulfilment of love, or else will be consumed, burned up, annihilated in its own failure. Yet God is never loved according to His worth by any creatures. And to the enlightened reason this is a great delight and satisfaction: that its God and its Beloved is so high and so rich that He transcends all created powers, and can be loved according to His merits by none save Himself.

This rich and enlightened man shall distribute gifts to all the angelic choirs, and all spirits, each in particular according to its merits, out of the richness of his God and out of the generosity of his own ground; which is illuminated and overflowing with great and wonderful gifts. He passes through all choirs, through all hierarchies and orders, and beholds how God dwells in all according to the merit of each. This enlightened man goes swiftly and in ghostly wise round and through all the heavenly hosts, rich and overflowing with charity, and enriching and inundating the whole celestial company with fresh glory out of the Richness and Abundance of the Trinity and Unity of the Divine Nature.

This is the first going out, towards God and towards all saints.

CHAPTER XLI

HE SHALL GO OUT TOWARDS ALL SINNERS

At times this same man shall descend towards sinners, with great compassion, and with generous mercy, and shall bring them before God with fervent devotion and with much prayer; bringing to God's remembrance all the good which He is, and all His power, and all that He has done for us, and has promised us, right as though He had forgotten all this: for God wills that we beseech Him. And charity shall obtain all that it desires; nevertheless it must not be stubborn and self-willed, but must leave all to the rich goodness and to the generosity of God: for God loves without measure, and herein the lover best finds his peace. Now, since this man bears a common love to all, he prays and beseeches God that His love and His mercy may flow forth towards Pagans and towards Jews and towards all unbelievers, that He may be loved and known and praised in heaven, and that our glory, our joy and our peace may spread to all the ends of the earth.

This is the second going out, towards sinners.

CHAPTER XLII

HE SHALL GO OUT TOWARDS HIS FRIENDS IN PURGATORY

At times the man shall behold his friends in purgatory, and shall consider their misery and their yearnings and their heavy pains. Then shall he pray and beseech the pity, the mercy, and the generosity of God; and shall

plead their good-will, and their great misery, and their
yearning after the rich goodness of God, and he shall
bring to God's remembrance that they died in love,
and that their only refuge is in His passion and mercy.

Now understand this : it may sometimes happen
that this enlightened man is specially urged of the
Spirit of God to pray for a certain thing, for some
sinner, or for some soul, or for some ghostly benefit,
in such a way that he feels and understands it to be
the work of the Holy Ghost, and not of his own choice,
or self-will, or nature.   Then the man sometimes
becomes so intense and so ardent in his prayer that he
receives in ghostly wise the answer that his prayer
has been heard.   And with the coming of this sign the
thrust of the Spirit and the prayer abate.

CHAPTER XLIII

HE SHALL GO OUT TOWARDS HIMSELF AND TOWARDS ALL GOOD MEN

Now the man shall go out towards himself and towards all men of good-will, and shall taste and behold
how that they are tied and bound together in love ;
and he shall beseech and pray God that He may let
His customary gifts flow forth, that thereby all may
be confirmed in His love and His eternal worship.
This enlightened man shall faithfully and discreetly
teach and instruct, reprove and serve, all men ; for
he bears in him a love towards all.   And thereby is
he a mediator between God and all men.   And then
he shall turn wholly inwards upon himself with all
the saints and with all the just, and possess in peace

the unity of his spirit, and therewith the most high Unity of God, wherein all spirits rest. This is a true ghostly life; for all the degrees and all the virtues, inward as well as outward, and the highest powers of the soul, are supernaturally adorned by it in a right and profitable way.

CHAPTER XLIV

SHOWING HOW WE MAY RECOGNISE THOSE MEN WHO FAIL IN CHARITY TO ALL

THERE are some men who are very subtle in words, and skilful in showing forth high things, and yet do not enjoy this enlightened condition, neither this common and generous charity. In order that these men may learn to know themselves, and also may be known of others, I will distinguish them by three signs. By the first sign they may be known of themselves, and by the two others they may be recognised of all men of understanding.

The first sign: Whereas the enlightened man, by virtue of the Divine light, is simple and stable and free from curious considerations, these others are manifold and restless and full of subtle reasonings and reflections; and they do not taste inward unity, nor the satisfaction which is without images. And by this they may know themselves.

The second sign: Whereas the enlightened man possesses a wisdom inpoured by God, wherein he knows and distinguishes the truth without effort, these men have shrewd and sudden notions, with which they work in their imagination, and which they display and develop with much cunning. But their ground is barren and they cannot bring forth fruitful doctrine. Their doctrines are manifold, they are concerned with outward things and addressed to the understanding. And thereby inward men are troubled, hindered, and led astray. They neither lead nor point to unity ; but they teach subtle observations in multiplicity. Such people hold obstinately to their own doctrine and opinion, even though another opinion be as good as their own. And they are idle and careless as regards all virtues. Spiritual pride is in all their being. This is the second sign.

The third sign : Whereas the enlightened and loving man flows forth in love towards all in heaven and on earth, as you have heard, this other man sets himself apart in all things. He thinks himself to be the wisest and the best of all ; and desires that others should think highly of him and his teaching. All those whom he does not teach and advise, all those who do not follow his way of life and do not cling to him as their master, these seem to him to be sunk in error. He is large and spacious in satisfying his bodily needs, and little faults do not count heavily with him. This man is neither just, nor humble, nor generous, nor a servant of the poor, nor inward, nor fervent, nor does he feel the love of God. He knows neither God, nor his own being, in the way of true virtue. This is the third sign.

Mark these, and study them, and cast them out of yourselves, and out of all men in whom you remark them ; but condemn no one for such things unless it be that they have proved it by their deeds, for this would soil your heart and would hinder it in the knowledge of Divine truth.

CHAPTER XLV

HOW CHRIST WAS, IS, AND EVER WILL BE THE LOVER OF ALL

IN order that we shall possess and desire this state of being common to all above the other conditions of which we have spoken (because this state is the highest of all) we shall take as a model Christ, Who was, and is, and eternally shall remain common to all; for He was sent down to earth for the common benefit of all men who would turn to Him.

Yet He Himself says that He is not sent but unto the lost sheep of the house of Israel. These, however, are not only the Jews, but all those who shall see God in eternity. These belong to the house of Israel, and no one else; for the Jews despised the Gospel, and the Heathen entered and received it. And so all Israel, that is to say, all the eternally chosen, shall be saved.

Now mark how Christ gave Himself to all in perfect loyalty. His inward and sublime prayer flowed forth towards His Father, and it was a prayer for all in common who desired to be saved. Christ was common to all in love, in teaching, in tender consolation, in generous gifts, in merciful forgiveness. His soul and His body, His life and His death and His ministry were, and are, common to all. His sacraments and His gifts are common to all. Christ never took any food or drink, nor anything that His body needed, without intending by it the common good of all those who shall be saved, even unto the last day. Christ had nothing particular and of his own, but everything in common, body and soul, mother and disciples, cloak and tunic. He ate and He drank for our sake ;

He lived and He died for our sake. His pains and His sorrows and His miseries were of His own and for Him only; but the fruits and the profit which came forth from them are common to all. And the glory of His merits shall be common to all in eternity.

CHAPTER XLVI

REPROVING ALL THOSE WHO LIVE ON SPIRITUAL GOODS IN AN INORDINATE MANNER

Now Christ left His treasure and His revenue here on earth. These are the seven sacraments and the outward goods of Holy Church, which He has gotten through His death, and which, therefore, should be in common. And His servants, who live thereon, should therefore be in common. All those who live on alms, and are in the ecclesiastical state, should be in common, at least in their prayers: and especially all religious who live in cloisters and in cells. In the beginning of Holy Church and of our Faith, popes, bishops, and priests, were all in common; for they went out and converted the folk, and established Holy Church and our Faith, and sealed them with their blood and with their death. These men were simple and one-fold, and they had steadfast peace in the unity of the spirit. And they were enlightened with godly wisdom, rich and overflowing with faith and with love towards God and towards all men. But now, notwithstanding, it is become wholly otherwise; for those who to-day possess the heritage and the revenue which were given to those others out of love and because of their holiness, are unstable of soul, and restless, and in

multiplicity; for they have altogether turned towards
the world, and do not thoroughly apprehend in their
ground those things and that business which they
have in hand. That is why they pray with their
lips; but their heart does not savour the meaning,
that is to say, it does not feel the secret wonder which
is hidden in Scripture, and in the sacraments, and in
their office. And therefore they are coarse and dull,
and are not enlightened by the Divine truth, and they
often seek food and drink and ease of body without
moderation: would to God they were at least clean
of fleshly sins! As long as they live thus, they shall
never be enlightened; and whereas those others were
generous, and overflowing with charity, and kept
nothing for themselves, these are now greedy and
avaricious, and deny themselves nothing. All this
is contrary and unlike to the saints, and to that
common way of which we have spoken. I speak of
the general state of things: let each prove himself,
and teach and reprove himself, if needs be; and, if
not, let him rejoice and rest in peace in his clean
conscience, and serve and praise God, for the good of
himself and of all men, and for the glory of God.

CHAPTER XLVII

SHOWING HOW CHRIST HAS GIVEN HIMSELF TO ALL IN COMMON IN THE SACRAMENT OF THE ALTAR

As I will specially praise and glorify this state of
being in common, so I find another special treasure
which Christ has left in Holy Church to all good men;
in His supper upon the high feast of the Passover

when Christ knew that He would pass from this exile to His father, after He had eaten of the Paschal Lamb with His disciples, and the ancient law had been fulfilled. At the end of the meal and of the feast, He desired to give to them a dish of singular excellence, which He had long wished to do. And herewith He willed to make an end of the ancient law and begin the new. And He took bread in His holy and venerable hands, and consecrated His sacred Body, and after that His sacred Blood ; and He gave them both to all His disciples, and left them to all good men in common for their eternal profit. This gift and this excellent dish rejoice and adorn all high festivals and all banquets, in heaven and on earth. In this gift Christ gives Himself to us in three ways. He gives us His Flesh and His Blood and His bodily life, glorified and full of joy and sweetness ; He gives us His spirit with its highest powers, full of glory and gifts, truth and righteousness ; and He gives us His personality through that Divine Light which raises His spirit and all enlightened spirits into the most high and fruitive unity.

Now Christ desires that we shall remember Him so often as we consecrate, offer, and receive His Body. Consider now how we shall remember Him. We shall mark and behold how Christ inclines Himself towards us with loving affection, with great desire, and with yearning delight, and with a warm and tender outpouring of Himself into our bodily nature. For He gives us that which He has in common with our manhood, that is, His Flesh and His Blood, and His bodily nature. We shall also mark and behold that precious body martyred, pierced and wounded for our sake, because of His love and His faithfulness towards us.

Herewith we are adorned and nourished in the lower part of our manhood. In this most high gift of the Sacrament He also gives us His spirit, full of glory and rich gifts of virtue, and unspeakable marvels of charity and nobleness. And herewith we are nourished and adorned and enlightened in the unity of our spirit and in the higher powers, through the indwelling of Christ with all His riches. Moreover He gives us in the Sacrament of the Altar His most high personality in incomprehensible splendour. And through this we are lifted up to and united with the Father, and the Father receives His adopted sons together with His natural Son, and thus we enter into our inheritance of the Godhead in eternal blessedness.

When a man has worthily recollected and considered these things, then he shall go out to meet Christ in the same way in which Christ comes to him. He shall lift himself up to receive Christ with his heart, with his desire, with sensible love, with all his powers, and with a joyful craving. For even thus does Christ receive Himself. And this craving cannot be too great; for then our nature receives its own nature, that is, the glorified manhood of Christ, full of joy and worth. Therefore I would that a man, in thus receiving, should melt and flow forth in desire, in joy, and in delight: for he embraces and is united with Him who is the fairest, the most gracious and most lovable of all the children of men. In this yearning devotion, and in these delights, many a great benefit has been bestowed upon men, and many a secret and hidden wonder of the rich treasures of God has been revealed and disclosed to them. When a man, in thus receiving, bethinks himself of the martyrdom and the sufferings of this precious Body of Christ,

which he receives, then he may sometimes rise into
such loving devotion and such sensible compassion
that he desires to be nailed with Christ to the cross,
and longs to shed his heart's blood for the glory of
Christ.   And he presses into the wounds and into
the open heart of Christ, his Saviour.   In this exercise
many a revelation and many a benefit have often
been bestowed upon men.

This sensible love and compassion, and the power
of the imagination united with the inward contemplation of the wounds of Christ, may be so great, that
the man thinks that he feels the wounds and the
bruises of Christ in his own heart and in all his limbs.
And if any man could indeed in any way receive the
stigmata of our Lord, it would be such a man as this.
And herewith we satisfy Christ as regards the lower
part of His manhood.

We shall also dwell in the unity of our spirit and
should flow forth with an ample love in heaven and
on earth, with clear discernment.   And by this we
bear some resemblance to Christ as regards the spirit,
and give Him satisfaction.

We shall also, through the personality of Christ,
with simplicity of intention and with fruitive love,
transcend ourselves, and also the created being of
Christ, and rest in our inheritance, that is, in the
Divine Being in eternity.   This Christ always desires
to give us in ghostly wise, whenever we so exercise
ourselves and make ourselves in readiness for Him.
And He desires that we shall receive Him both in a
sacramental and a spiritual way, as is meet and right
and as reason demands.   Though a man may not
always have such feelings and such desires, if he
intend the praise of God and His glory, and the

increase of his own being and blessedness, he may go freely to the table of the Lord, if his conscience be clean from mortal sin.

CHAPTER XLVIII

OF THE UNITY OF THE DIVINE NATURE IN THE TRINITY OF THE PERSONS

THE most high and superessential Unity of the Divine Nature, where the Father and the Son possess Their nature in the unity of the Holy Ghost—above the comprehension and understanding of all our powers, in the naked being of our spirit—is a supernal stillness, wherein God broods above all creatures in the created light. This most high Unity of the Divine Nature is living and fruitful; for, out of this same Unity, the Eternal Word is incessantly born of the Father. And, through this birth, the Father knows the Son; and, in the Son, all things. And the Son knows the Father; and all things in the Father. For they are one Simple Nature. From this mutual contemplation of the Father and the Son, in the eternal radiance, there flow forth an eternal content and a fathomless love, and that is the Holy Ghost. And through the Holy Ghost, and through the Eternal Wisdom, God inclines Himself towards each creature in particular, and lovingly endows and enkindles each one, according to its worth and the state into which it has been put and to which it has been destined by its virtues and by the Eternal Providence of God. And thereby all good spirits, in heaven and on earth, are moved to virtue and righteousness.

CHAPTER XLIX

SHOWING HOW GOD POSSESSES AND MOVES THE SOUL
BOTH IN A NATURAL AND A SUPERNATURAL WAY

Now mark well : I will show you an image of this.
God has created the highest heaven, a pure and simple
Radiance, which enrings and encloses all the heavens
and all bodily and material things that God has ever
created ; for it is an outward dwelling-place and a
kingdom of God and His saints, full of glory and
eternal joy.   Now since this heaven is an unmingled
Radiance, there is here neither time, nor space, nor
movement, nor any change ; for it is immovable and
unchangeable above all things.   The sphere which
is nearest to this glowing heaven is called the First
Movement.   For here all movement arises from the
highest heaven, by the Power of God.   From this
movement the firmament and all planets derive their
courses.   And, through it, all creatures live and
grow, each according to its kind.   Now understand this well : so likewise the essence of the soul
is a ghostly kingdom of God, full of Divine radiance,
transcending all our powers, except they be in that
simplified state of which I will not speak now.   Behold, in regard to the essence of the soul, wherein
God reigns, the unity of our spirit is like to the First
Movement ; for, in this unity, the spirit is moved
from above by the power of God, both naturally and
supernaturally.   For we have nothing of our own,
neither in nature, nor above nature.   And this stirring of God, when it is supernatural, is the first and
principle cause of all virtues.   And through this
stirring of God, there are given to some men the

seven gifts of the Holy Ghost, like to the seven planets, which illuminate and make fruitful the whole life of man. This is the way in which God possesses the essential unity of our spirit as His kingdom ; and in which He works and flows forth with His gifts into our potential unity and into all our powers.

CHAPTER L

SHOWING HOW A MAN SHOULD BE ADORNED
IF HE IS TO RECEIVE THE MOST INWARD EXERCISE

Now consider diligently how we can acquire and possess the most inward exercise of our spirit in the created light. The man who is well adorned with the moral virtues of the outward life, and has risen into nobility and divine peace by inward practices; he possesses the unity of the spirit, enlightened by supernatural wisdom, flowing forth in generous love toward heaven and earth and lifting itself up by its reverence and its merits, and flowing back into that very ground, the most high Unity of God, from which all things proceed. For each creature, according to whether it has received more or less from God, has more or less of ascending love and inward tendency towards its origin ; for God and all His gifts invite us into Him, and through charity and the virtues and resemblance, we desire to enter into Him.

CHAPTER LI

OF THE THIRD COMING OF CHRIST

THROUGH this loving inclination of God, and His inward working in the unity of our spirit, and further through our glowing love and the pressing of all our powers together into the very unity in which God dwells, there arises the third coming of Christ in inward working. And this is an inward touch or stirring of Christ in His Divine brightness, in the inmost part of our spirit. The second coming, of which we have spoken, we have likened to a fountain, pouring forth in three rills. But this coming we will liken to the duct which feeds the fountain. For there is no rill without a fountain; and no fountain without a living duct. So likewise the grace of God flows forth like rills into the higher powers, and impels and enkindles a man in all virtue. And this grace springs up within the unity of our spirit like a fountain, and falls back again into that same unity whence it arises; even as a living and gushing spring which comes forth from the living ground of the Divine Richness, where neither faithfulness nor grace can ever fail. And this is the touch which I mean. And the creature passively endures this touch. For here there is a union of the higher powers within the unity of the spirit, above the multiplicity of all the virtues, and here no one works save God alone, in untrammelled goodness; which is the cause of all our virtues and of all blessedness. In the unity of the spirit, into which this duct gushes forth, one is above activity and above reason, though not without reason. For the enlightened reason, and especially the power of love, feels this touch ; and reason cannot understand, nor can it comprehend, the way or the means of this touch, how or what it is, for it is a working of God, the upspringing and the inrushing of all graces and gifts, and the last intermediary between God and the creature. And above this touch, in the still being of the spirit, there broods an incomprehensible Brightness. And that is the most high Trinity whence this touch proceeds. There God lives and reigns in the spirit, and the spirit in God.

CHAPTER LII

SHOWING HOW THE SPIRIT GOES OUT THROUGH THE DIVINE STIRRING

Now, through this touch, Christ says inwardly within the spirit : Go YE OUT with practices in conformity with this touch. For this deep touch draws and invites our spirit to the most inward practices which a creature is able to fulfil in a creaturely way in the created light. Here the spirit raises itself, through the power of love, above all works, into the unity where this life-giving spring or touch gushes forth. And this touch invites the understanding to know God in His brightness, and it draws and invites the power of love to enjoy God without intermediary. And this the loving spirit desires to do, both in a natural and a supernatural way, above all other things. By means of the enlightened reason the spirit lifts itself up in inward observation, and it beholds and observes the most inward part of itself, where this touch lives. Here reason and every created light fail and can go no further. For the Supernal Brightness brooding over all, which gives rise to this touch, blinds in its coming every created sight; for it is abysmal. And all understanding in the created light is here like the eyes of a bat in the light of the sun. Yet the spirit is continually invited and urged anew by God and by itself to sound and to know that which is stirring these deeps, and what God is, and what this touch is. And the enlightened reason ever asks anew, whence this comes, and ever seeks to explore further, that it may follow back this stream of honey to its source. But in this it is, on the first day, as wise as it shall ever be. And this is why reason and all observation say: " I know not what it is," for the Supernal Brightness brooding over all, strikes back all understanding and blinds it whenever they meet.

So God abides in His brightness above all spirits who are in heaven and on earth. And those who have pierced through their ground by means of the virtues and inward practices, to their source, that is, to the door of eternal life, may feel this touch. There the Brightness of God shines so mightily that reason and all understanding fail and can go no further, but must be overcome and give way before the incomprehensible Brightness of God. But when the spirit feels this in its ground, then, though its reason and understanding fail before the Divine Brightness, and must remain outside the door, the power of love desires to go forward; for it too, like the understanding, has been invited and urged. And it is blind and desires fruition; and fruition abides more in tasting and feeling than in understanding. Therefore would love go forward, whilst understanding stays outside.

CHAPTER LIII

OF AN ETERNAL HUNGER FOR GOD

HERE there begins an eternal hunger, which shall never more be satisfied ; it is an inward craving and hankering of the loving power and the created spirit after an uncreated Good. And since the spirit longs for fruition, and is invited and urged thereto by God, it must always desire its fulfilment. Behold, here there begins an eternal craving and continual yearning in eternal insatiableness. All such are the poorest of all men living ; for they are avid and greedy, and their hunger is insatiable. Whatever they eat or drink, they shall never be satisfied, for this hunger is eternal. For a created vessel cannot contain an uncreated Good : and hence there is here an eternal, hungry craving without satisfaction, and God poured forth above all and yet staying it not. Here are great dishes of food and drink, of which no one knows save he who tastes them : but full satisfaction in fruition is the dish which is lacking there, and therefore this hunger is ever renewed. Yet, in the touch, rivers of honey, full of all delights, flow forth ; for the spirit tastes these riches in all the ways which it can conceive and apprehend ; but all this is in a creaturely way and below God, and hence there remains an eternal hunger and impatience. Though God gave to such a man all the gifts which are possessed by all the saints, and everything that He is able to give, but withheld Himself, the gaping desire of the spirit would remain hungry and unsatisfied. The inward stirring and touching of God makes us hungry and yearning ; for the Spirit of God hunts our spirit : and the more it touches it, the greater our hunger and our craving. And this is the life of love in its highest working, above reason and above understanding ; for reason can here neither give nor take away from love, for our love is touched by the Divine love. And as I understand it, here there can never more be separation from God. God's touch within us, forasmuch as we feel it, and our own loving craving, these are both created and creaturely ; and therefore they may grow and increase as long as we live.

CHAPTER LIV

OF A LOVING STRIFE BETWEEN THE SPIRIT OF GOD AND OUR SPIRIT

IN this storm of love two spirits strive together : the spirit of God and our own spirit. God, through the Holy Ghost, inclines Himself towards us ; and, thereby, we are touched in love. And our spirit, by God's working and by the power of love, presses and inclines itself into God : and, thereby, God is touched. From these two contacts there arises the strife of love, at the very deeps of this meeting ; and in that most inward and ardent encounter, each spirit is deeply wounded by love. These two spirits, that is, our own spirit and the Spirit of God, sparkle and shine one into the other, and each shows to the other its face. This makes each of the spirits yearn for the other in love. Each demands of the other all that it is ; and each offers to the other all that it is and invites it to all that it is. This makes the lovers melt into each other. God's touch and His gifts, our loving craving and our giving back : these fulfil love. This flux and reflux causes the fountain of love to brim over : and thus the touch of God and our loving craving become one simple love. Here man is possessed by love, so that he must forget himself and God, and knows and can do nothing but love. Thereby the spirit is burned up in the fire of love, and enters so deeply into the touch of God, that it is overcome in all its cravings, and turned to nought in all its works, and empties itself ; above all surrender becoming very love. And it possesses, above all virtues, the inmost part of its created being, where every creaturely work begins and ends. Such is love in itself, foundation and origin of all virtues.

CHAPTER LV

OF THE FRUITFUL WORKS OF THE SPIRIT, THE WHICH ARE ETERNAL

Now our spirit and this love are living and fruitful in virtues ; and for this reason the powers can no longer remain idle in the unity of the spirit. For the incomprehensible brightness of God and His boundless love brood above the spirit, and touch the loving power ; and the spirit goes forth once more into its works, but with a more sublime and inward striving than ever before. And the more noble and inward it is, the more quickly it is spent and brought to nought in love, and goes forth once more into fresh works. And this is heavenly love. For ever does the craving spirit yearn to eat and to swallow God ;

but itself is swallowed up in the touch of God, and fails in all its works. For the highest powers are made one in the unity of the spirit. Here are grace and love in their essence, above all works; for here is the source of charity and every virtue. Here there is an eternal outflow into charity and the virtues, and an eternal return with inward hunger for the taste of God, and an eternal dwelling within in pure love. And all this is in a creaturely way, and below God; it is the most inward exercise which one can perform in the created light, in heaven and on earth; and above it there is nothing but the God-seeing life in the Divine light and in the God-like way. In this exercise one cannot go astray, nor can one be deceived; and it begins in grace, and shall for ever last in glory.

CHAPTER LVI

SHOWING THE WAY IN WHICH WE SHALL MEET GOD IN A GHOSTLY MANNER BOTH WITH AND WITHOUT MEANS

Now I have shown you how the free and uplifted man becomes, through the grace of God, seeing in his inward practices. And we see that this is the first point which Christ demands and desires of us, where He says: BEHOLD. As to the second and third points, wherein He says: THE BRIDEGROOM COMETH, and: GO YE OUT, I have shown you the three ways of the inward coming of Christ; and further that the first coming has four degrees, and how we are to go out with practices answering to each way in which

God inwardly enkindles, teaches, and moves us. Now we must consider the fourth point, which is the last. This is the meeting with Christ our Bridegroom. For all our inward and ghostly vision, in grace or in glory, and all our going out in the virtues, in whatsoever practices this be done, it is all for the sake of a meeting and a union with Christ our Bridegroom : for He is our eternal rest and the end and wage of all our labour.

You know that every meeting is a coming together of two persons, who come from different places, which are separated from, and opposite to, each other. Now Christ comes from above as a Lord and generous Giver, who can do all things. And we come from below as the poor servants, who can do nothing of ourselves, but have need of everything. The coming of Christ to us is from within outwards, and we go towards Him from without inwards ; and this is why a ghostly meeting must here take place. And this coming and this meeting of ourselves and Christ takes place in two ways, to wit, with means and without means.

CHAPTER LVII

OF THE ESSENTIAL MEETING WITH GOD WITHOUT MEANS IN THE NAKEDNESS OF OUR NATURE

Now understand and mark this well. The unity of our spirit has two conditions : it is essential, and it is active. You must know that the spirit, according to its essence, receives the coming of Christ in the nakedness of its nature, without means and without interruption. For the being and the life which we are in God, in our Eternal Image, and which we have within ourselves according to our essence, this is without means and indivisible. And this is why the spirit, in its inmost and highest part, that is in its naked nature, receives without interruption the impress of its Eternal Archetype, and the Divine Brightness; and is an eternal dwelling-place of God in which God dwells as an eternal Presence, and which He visits perpetually, with new comings and with new instreamings of the ever-renewed brightness of His eternal birth. For where He comes, there He is; and where He is, there He comes. And where He has never been, thereto He shall never come; for neither chance nor change are in Him. And everything in which He is, is in Him; for He never goes out of Himself. And this is why the spirit in its essence possesses God in the nakedness of its nature, as God does the spirit : for it lives in God and God in it. And it is able, in its highest part, to receive, without intermediary, the Brightness of God, and all that God can fulfil. And by means of the brightness of its Eternal Archetype, which shines in it essentially and personally, the spirit plunges itself and loses itself, as regards the highest part of its life,   in the Divine Being, and there abidingly possesses its eternal blessedness; and it flows forth again, through the eternal birth of the Son, together with all the other creatures, and is set in its created being by the free will of the Holy Trinity. And here it is like unto the image of the most high Trinity in Unity, in which it has been made. And, in its created being, it incessantly receives the impress of its Eternal Archetype, like a flawless mirror, in which the image remains steadfast, and in which the reflection is renewed without interruption by its ever-new reception in new light. This essential union of our spirit with God does not exist in itself, but it dwells in God, and it flows forth from God, and it depends upon God, and it returns to God as to its Eternal Origin.

And in this wise it has never been, nor ever shall be, separated from God ; for this union is within us by our naked nature, and, were this nature to be separated from God, it would fall into pure nothingness. And this union is above time and space, and is always and incessantly active according to the way of God. But our nature, forasmuch as it is indeed like unto God but in itself is creature, receives the impress of its Eternal Image passively. This is that nobleness which we possess by nature in the essential unity of our spirit, where it is united with God according to nature. This neither makes us holy nor blessed, for all men, whether good or evil, possess it within themselves ; but it is certainly the first cause of all holiness and all blessedness. This is the meeting and the union between God and our spirit in the nakedness of our nature.

CHAPTER LVIII

SHOWING HOW ONE IS LIKE UNTO GOD THROUGH GRACE
AND UNLIKE UNTO GOD THROUGH MORTAL SIN

Now consider this thought earnestly ; for if you understand well that which I will now tell you, and that which I have told you, you will have understood all the Divine truth which any creature can teach you, and far more besides. Otherwise does our spirit

keep itself in that same unity when it is conceived
as acting or working : for then it exists in itself as in
its created and personal being.   This is the source of
the higher powers, and here there are beginning and
end of all the creaturely works which are worked in
a creaturely way, both in nature and above nature.
Yet here the unity does not work forasmuch as it is
unity ; but all the powers of the soul, in what way
soever they work, derive their strength and their
power from their proper source, that is, from the unity
of the spirit, where it dwells in its personal being.

In this unity, the spirit must always either be like
unto God through grace and virtue, or unlike unto
God through mortal sin.   For, that man has been
made after the likeness of God, means that he has
been created in the grace of God ; the which grace
is a God-formed light, which shines through us
and makes us like to God ; and without this light,
which makes us God-like, we cannot be united with
God supernaturally, even though we cannot lose the
image of God nor our natural unity with Him.   If
we lose the likeness, that is, the grace of God, we are
damned.   And therefore, whenever God finds within
us some capacity for the reception of His grace, it is
His pleasure and His free goodness to make us, through
His gifts, full of life, and like unto Him.   This always
happens whenever we turn to Him with our whole
will ; for at that very moment, Christ comes to us
and in us, both with means and without means, that
is, with the virtues and above the virtues.   And He
impresses His image and His likeness in us, namely
Himself and His gifts : and He redeems us from sin,
and makes us free and like unto Himself.   And in
that same working, through which God redeems us

from sins, and makes us free and like unto Him through charity, the spirit immerses itself in fruitive love.

And here there take place a meeting and a union which are without means and above nature, and wherein our highest blessedness consists. Although all that He gives us from love and free goodness is natural to God, for us, according to our condition, it is accidental and supernatural. For before, we were strangers and unlike unto God; and afterwards, becoming like Him, have received union with God.

CHAPTER LIX

SHOWING HOW ONE POSSESSES GOD IN UNION AND REST, ABOVE ALL LIKENESS THROUGH GRACE

THIS meeting and this union, which the loving spirit achieves in God and possesses without means, must take place in the essential intuition, deeply hidden from our understanding; unless it be an effective understanding according to the way of simplicity.

In the fruition of this unity we shall rest evermore, above ourselves and above all things. From this unity, all gifts, both natural and supernatural, flow forth, and yet the loving spirit rests in this unity above all gifts; and here there is nothing but God, and the spirit united with God without means. In this unity we are taken possession of by the Holy Ghost, and we take possession of the Holy Ghost and the Father and the Son, and the whole Divine Nature: for God cannot be divided. And the fruitive tendency of the spirit, which seeks rest in God above all likeness, receives and possesses in a supernatural way, in its essential being, all that the spirit ever received in a natural way. All good men experience this; but *how* it is, this remains hidden from them all their life long if they do not become inward and empty of all creatures. In that very moment in which man turns away from sin, he is received by God in the essential unity of his own being, at the summit of his spirit, that he may rest in God, now and evermore. And he also receives grace, and likeness unto God, in the proper source of his powers, that he may evermore grow and increase in new virtues. And as long as this likeness endures in charity and in virtues, so long also endures the union in rest. And this cannot be lost save only by mortal sin.

CHAPTER LX

SHOWING HOW WE HAVE NEED OF THE GRACE OF GOD,
WHICH MAKES US LIKE UNTO GOD AND LEADS US
TO GOD WITHOUT MEANS

Now all holiness and all blessedness lie in this: that the spirit is led upwards, through likeness and by means of grace or glory, to rest in the essential unity. For the grace of God is the way by which we must always go, if we would enter into the naked essence in which God gives Himself with all His riches without means. And this is why the sinners and the damned spirits dwell in darkness; for they lack the grace of God, which should enlighten them, and lead them, and show them the way to the fruitive unity. Yet the essential being of the spirit is so noble, that even the damned cannot will their own annihilation. But sin builds up a barrier, and gives rise to such darkness and such unlikeness between the powers and the essence in which God lives, that the spirit cannot be united with its proper essence; which would be its own and its eternal rest, did sin not impede it. For whosoever lives without sin, he lives in likeness unto God, and in grace, and God is his own. And so we have need of grace, which casts out sin, and prepares the way, and makes our whole life fruitful. And this is why Christ always comes into us through means, that is, through grace and multifarious gifts; and we too go out towards Him through means, that is, through virtues and diverse practices. And the more inward gifts He gives and the more deeply He stirs us, the more inward and delightful are the workings of our spirit, as you have already heard in all the ways which have been shown forth before. And here there is a perpetual renewal; for God ever gives new gifts, and our spirit ever turns inward in such wise as it is invited and as is bestowed on it by God, and in that meeting it always receives a higher renewal. And thus one grows continually into a higher life. And this active meeting is altogether through means; for the gifts of God and our virtues and the activity of our spirit are the means. And these means are necessary for all men and all spirits: for, without the mediation of God's grace and a loving turning to Him in freedom, no creature shall ever be saved.

CHAPTER LXI

OF HOW GOD AND OUR SPIRIT VISIT EACH OTHER
IN THE UNITY AND IN THE LIKENESS

Now God sees the dwelling and the resting-place
which He has made within us and through us ; namely,
the unity and the likeness.   And He wills to visit
this unity without interruption, with a new coming
of His most high birth and with a rich pouring forth
of his fathomless love ; for He wills to dwell in bliss
within the loving spirit.   And He wills to visit the
likeness of our spirit with rich gifts, so that we become
more like unto Him and more enlightened in the
virtues.   Now it is Christ's will that we should dwell
and abide within the essential unity of our spirit, rich
with Him above all creaturely works and above all
virtues ; and that we should dwell actively in that same
unity, rich and fulfilled with virtues and heavenly
gifts.   And He wills that we shall visit that unity and
that likeness without interruption, by means of every
work which we do : for in every new " Now," God
is born in us, and from this most high birth the Holy
Ghost flows forth with all His gifts.   Therefore we
should go out to meet the gifts of God through the
likeness ; and the most high birth, through the unity.

CHAPTER LXII

SHOWING HOW WE SHOULD GO OUT TO MEET GOD
IN ALL OUR WORKS

Now mark how, in each of our works, we shall go
out to meet God, and shall increase our likeness unto

Him, and shall more nobly possess the fruitive unity. By every good work, how small soever it be, which is directed to God with love and with an upright and single intention, we earn a greater likeness, and eternal life in God. A single intention draws together the scattered powers into the unity of the spirit, and joins the spirit to God. A single intention is end, and beginning, and adornment, of all virtues. A single intention offers to God praise and honour and all virtues : and it pierces and passes through itself, and all the heavens, and all things, and finds God within the simple ground of its own being. That intention is single which aims only at God and in all things only at their connection with God. The single intention casts out hypocrisy and duplicity, and a man must possess it and practise it in all his works above all other things ; for it is this which keeps man in the presence of God, clear in understanding, diligent in virtue, and free from outward fear, both now and in the Day of Doom. Singleness of intention is the single eye of which Christ speaks, giving light to the whole body—that is, to the man's works and his whole life—and cleansing it of sin. Singleness of intention is the inward, enlightened, and loving tendency of the spirit ; it is the foundation of all ghostliness ; it includes in itself faith, hope, and charity, for it trusts in God and is faithful to Him. It casts nature underfoot, it establishes peace, it drives out ghostly discontent, and preserves fulness of life in all the virtues. And it gives peace and hope and boldness toward God, both now and in the Day of Doom.

Thus we shall dwell in the unity of the spirit, in grace and in likeness ; and shall always go out to meet God by means of the virtues, and offer up to Him with a simple intention our whole life and all our works; and thus in every work, and ever more and more, we shall increase our likeness. And thus we rise up out of the ground of our single intention, and pass through ourselves and go out to meet God without means, and rest in Him in the abyss of simplicity : there we possess that heritage which has been prepared for us from all eternity. All ghostly life and all works of virtue consist in the Divine likeness and in singleness of intention; and all their supreme rest consists in simplicity above all likeness. Nevertheless, one spirit surpasses another in virtue and in likeness, and each possess its own proper being in itself, according to the degree of its nobleness. And God suffices each one in particular, and each one, according to the measure of his love, seeks God in the ground of his spirit ; both here and in eternity.

CHAPTER LXIII

OF THE ORDERING OF ALL THE VIRTUES THROUGH THE SEVEN GIFTS OF THE HOLY GHOST

Now consider the order and the degrees of all the virtues and of all holiness, with which we should go out to meet God through resemblance ; that so we may rest with Him in the unity.

THE GIFT OF FEAR

When a man lives in the Fear of God, in the moral virtues and in outward works ; and when he is obedient and submissive to Holy Church and to the

Divine commandments, and when he is ready and willing in simplicity of intention to do all good things : then he is like unto God, through faithfulness, and through the gathering of his will into the will of God, both in doing and in leaving undone. And he rests in God, above likeness ; for through faithfulness and singleness of intention, he fulfils the will of God, more or less according to the measure of his likeness ; and through love, he rests in his Beloved above likeness.

THE GIFT OF PIETY

And if he exerts himself well in that which he has received from God, then God bestows upon him the spirit of Piety and Mercy. Thus he becomes gentle of heart, meek and merciful. And thereby he becomes more full of life and more like to God, and feels himself to be resting more in God, and to be broader and deeper in virtue than before. And he savours this likeness and this rest so much the better, the more his resemblance is increased.

THE GIFT OF KNOWLEDGE

And if he here exerts himself well, with great zeal, and with a single intention, and fights all that which is opposed to the virtues ; this man receives the third gift, which is Knowledge and Discretion. Thus he becomes reasonable and discerning, and knows what to do and what to leave undone, and where he must give and where he must take away. And through simplicity of intention and godly love, this man rests in God above himself in the unity ; and he possesses himself in likeness, and he possesses all his works with a greater delight, because he is obedient and submissive to the Father, and has reason and discernment through the Son, and is gentle and merciful through the Holy Ghost. And thus he bears a resemblance unto the Holy Trinity ; and he rests in God, through his love and the simplicity of his intention. And herein the whole of the active life consists. Thus a man should exert himself with great zeal, and should follow his single intention with reason and discernment. And he must beware of all that is opposed to the virtues, and must ever bow himself down in humility at the feet of Christ : and in this way he will grow ever more and more in virtue and in resemblance ; and if he keeps himself thus, he cannot err. Yet according to this way, he still remains in the active life. For if a man practises and clings to the activities of the heart and the diversity of works, more than to the ground and reason of all works ; and if he busies himself more with the practice of the sacraments, with their forms and outward symbols, than with the ground and the truth which are signified thereby : so he shall ever remain an outward man. But he shall be saved by his good works and his simplicity of intention.

THE GIFT OF STRENGTH

And therefore, if a man wishes to come nearer to God, and to exalt his practice and his life, he must proceed from the works to their reason, and from the forms to the truth ; thereby he shall become master of his works, and shall know truth, and shall come into the inward life. And God gives him the fourth gift, which is the spirit of Strength : and thus he shall

be able to overcome joy and grief, profit and loss,
hope and care in earthly things, together with all
kinds of hindrances and all multiplicity. And thus
he becomes free and detached from all creatures.
When a man has become free from all creaturely
images, he is master of himself, and easily and
without labour becomes inward and recollected ;
and turns freely and without hindrance to God, with
fervent devotion, with lofty desire, with thanksgiving
and praise, and with a single intention. Thus he
enters into fruition of all his deeds and his whole life,
inward and outward ; for he stands before the throne
of the Holy Trinity, and often receives inward consolation and sweetness from God. For he who serves
at such a table with thanksgiving and praise, and with
inward reverence, often drinks of the wine, and often
eats of that which is left, and of the crumbs which
fall from the Lord's table : and he continually possesses inward peace, through the singleness of his
intention. And if he will abide steadfastly before
God in thanksgiving and praise, and with uplifted
purpose, the spirit of Strength is doubled within him ;
for then he no longer loses himself in bodily desires,
in longings after consolation or sweetness, nor in any
other gift of God, nor in rest and peace of the heart.
But he will forego all gifts and every consolation, if
so be that he may find Him Whom he loves. In this
way he is strong who abandons and overcomes the
unrest of the heart and earthly things ; and doubly
strong is he who also foregoes and overpasses every
consolation and heavenly gift. Thus a man transcends all creatures, and possesses himself, powerful
and free, through the gift of spiritual Strength.

THE GIFT OF COUNSEL

When, therefore, no creature can either overcome
or impede a man from persisting in his single and
upward-striving intention; and when through this
Strength he is steadfast in praising God, seeking and
meaning God above all His gifts, then God bestows
upon him the fifth gift, which is the gift of Counsel.
In this gift the Father draws the man inwardly, and
calls him to His right hand, with the chosen in His
unity. And the Son says in ghostly wise within
him : " Follow Me to My Father : ONE THING IS NEED-
FUL." And the Holy Ghost makes the heart expand
and flame up in fiery love. And thence comes
the life of loving tumult and inward restlessness ;
for, in him who listens to this counsel, there arises a
storm of love, and nothing can satisfy him save God
alone. And therefore he abandons himself and all
things, that he may find Him in Whom he lives and
in Whom all things are one. Here the man should
have God in mind in a simple way, and should master
himself by means of the reason, and should renounce
all self-will, and should await in freedom the unity
which he desires, until the day when it is God's pleasure
to give it. Thus the spirit of Counsel works in him
in two ways : for that man is great, and follows the
precept and counsel of God, who abandons himself
and all things, and says, with an insatiable, impetuous
and burning love : THY KINGDOM COME. But that
man is greater still, and follows still better the counsel
of God, who overcomes his own self-will, and renounces
it in love, and says unto God with reverent sub-
mission : THY WILL BE DONE in all things and not
my will. When Christ our dear Lord approached

His passion, He said those very words unto His Father, in humble abnegation of Himself; and they were to Him the most happy, and to us the most wholesome, and to the Father the most lovable, and to the devil the most terrible, words which Christ ever spoke; for, by His renunciation of self-will according to His manhood, we are all saved. In this way the will of God now becomes to the loving and humble man the highest joy, and the greatest desire of his ghostly feelings: even though this will should lead him to hell, which is impossible. And here nature is cast down into the depths, and God is exalted most highly; and this man becomes capable of receiving all the gifts of God; for he has denied himself, and has renounced his own self, and has given all for all. And he therefore asks nothing and wills nothing but that which God wishes to give him. That which God wills, this is his joy; and he who surrenders himself to God in love is the most free of all men living. He lives without care, for God cannot lose that which is His.

Now mark this: although God knows all hearts, yet such a man is often tempted and tried of Him, whether he is able to renounce himself in freedom: and by this, he may then become enlightened, and may live for the glory of God and also for his own salvation. And that is why God sometimes takes him from His right hand to His left, from heaven into hell, from all blessedness into great misery; so that it seems to him as though he were forsaken and despised of God and of all creatures. If, then, he has formerly renounced himself and his own will in love and in joy, so that he sought not himself but the good pleasure of God, he will easily renounce himself also

in pains and misery, so that in these too he will seek
not himself but always the glory of God. He who is
willing to work great things is willing also to suffer
great things ; but to bear and to suffer in resignation
is nobler and more pleasing to God, and more satisfying to our spirit, than to work great things in
a like resignation, for it is more contrary to
our nature. And this is why our spirit is more
exalted and our nature more cast down by grievous
suffering than by great works done with equal love.
When a man maintains himself in this resignation,
without any other preference, right as one who neither
wills nor knows anything else, then he possesses the
spirit of Counsel in two ways ; for he satisfies the
will and the counsel of God in his working and his
suffering, by self-surrender, and by submissive obedience. And his nature is adorned most gloriously :
and he is capable of being enlightened according to
the Spirit.

THE GIFT OF UNDERSTANDING

And therefore God gives him the sixth gift, which
is the spirit of Understanding. This gift we have
already likened to a fountain with three rills ; for it
establishes our spirit in the unity, it reveals Truth,
and it brings forth a wide and general love. This
gift may also be likened to sunshine, for by its shining
the sun fills the air with a simple brightness and
lights all forms, and shows the distinctions of all
colours. And thereby it shows forth its own power ;
and its heat is common to the whole world, bringing
forth fruits and useful things. So likewise does the
first ray of this gift bring about simplicity within

the spirit. And this simplicity is penetrated by a particular radiance even as the air of the heavens by the splendour of the sun. For the grace of God, which is the ground of all gifts, maintains itself essentially like to a simple light in our potential understanding : and, by means of this simple light our spirit is made stable and onefold and enlightened, and fulfilled of grace and Divine gifts : and here it is like unto God through grace and Divine love. And since the spirit is now like unto God, and means and loves God alone above all gifts, it will no longer be satisfied by likeness, nor by a created brightness ; for it has both by nature and above nature a primal tendency towards the Abysmal Being from which it has flowed forth. And the Unity of the Divine Being eternally draws back all likeness into its unity. And here the spirit is enkindled into fruition, and it melts into God as into its eternal rest ; for the grace of God is to God even as the sunshine is to the sun, and the grace of God is the means and the way which leads us to God. And for this reason it shines within us in simplicity, and makes us deiform, that is, like unto God. And this likeness perpetually merges itself in God, and dies in God, and becomes one with God, and remains one ; for charity makes us one with God, and causes us to remain one and to dwell in the One. Nevertheless we keep the eternal likeness in the light of grace or of glory; thereby we possess ourselves actively in charity and in the virtues. And we keep the union with God, above our activity, in the nakedness of our spirit, in the Divine light, where we possess God in rest, above all virtues. For charity in the likeness must ever be at work ; and union with God in fruitive love must ever be at rest. And this is the working of love ; for in one " Now " and at the same time love works and rests in its Beloved. And the one is strengthened by the other ; for the higher the love, the greater the rest ; and the greater the rest, the deeper the love ; for the one lives in the other, and whosoever loves not, rests not, and whosoever rests not, loves not. And yet, some good men think that they neither love nor rest in God ; and this thought itself comes from love. Because they desire to love more than they can, it seems to them that their love falls short. And yet in this work they taste love and rest ; for none save the resigned, emptied and enlightened man can understand how one may love in labour and rest in fruition. Yet every lover is one with God in rest, and like unto God in the works of love ; for God in His most high nature, of which we bear the likeness, dwells in fruition in eternal rest according to His Essential Unity, but works in eternal activity according to the Trinity : and the one is the perfection of the other ; for rest abides in the Unity, and work in the Trinity. And thus they dwell together throughout eternity. And, therefore, if a man is to taste of God, he must love ; and if he will love, then he may taste. But if he lets himself be satisfied with other things, he shall not be able to taste what God is. And therefore we must possess ourselves in simplicity, in virtue, and in likeness, and God above ourselves through love in rest and unity. And this is the first way in which the man who is common to all is made stable.

When the air is fulfilled with the brightness of the sun, the beauty and the wealth of the whole world are revealed, and the eyes of men become enlightened and rejoice in the manifold diversity of

colours. And so it is, when we are onefold within
ourselves, and our power of understanding is enlightened and the Spirit of Understanding shines
through it. Then we can become aware of the high
attributes which are in God, and which are the causes
of all the works which flow forth from Him. Although
all men may understand the works, and God through
His works; yet no one can truly understand, neither
in their appearance nor in their reality, the attributes
of the works of God as they are in their ground, save
by means of this gift. For this teaches us to seek out
and to recognise our own nobleness, and it gives us the
power to discern the virtues and all practices, and the
way in which we should live without error in accord-
ance with eternal Truth : and he who is enlightened by
it can dwell in the spirit, and can, with enlightened
reason, rightly apprehend and understand all things
in heaven and on earth. And therefore such a one
walks in heaven, and beholds and apprehends with all
saints the nobility of his Beloved, His incomprehensible height, His abysmal depth, length and breadth,
wisdom and truth, His bounty and His unspeakable
generosity, and all those loveworthy attributes which
are in God our Lover without number, and without
limit in His most high nature : for all this is He
Himself. Then that enlightened man lowers his
eyes, and beholds himself and all other men and all
creatures ; and observes how God in His free generosity has created them in nature and endowed them
in many ways, and how, above nature, it is His
pleasure to endow them and to enrich them with
Himself, if they will but seek and desire Him. All
such reasoning observation of the manifold diversities
of the Divine riches rejoices our spirit, if, through

Divine love, we have died unto ourselves in God, and if we live and walk in the spirit, and taste of the things which are eternal. This gift of Understanding shows us the unity which we possess in God through the fruitive immersion of love, and also the likeness to God which we have in ourselves through charity and the works of virtue. And it gives to us light and brightness in which we can walk with discernment in the ways of the spirit, and can seek out and recognise God in ghostly similitudes, and also ourselves, and all things according to the mode and the measure of that light and according to the will of God and the greater nobility of our understanding. This is the second degree in which the man who is common to all may be enlightened.

According to the measure in which the air is irradiated by the brightness of the sun, so too the heat increases and brings all things to fruitfulness. When our reason and understanding are so enlightened, that they can recognise and distinguish Divine truth, then the will, that is, the power of love, grows hotter and streams forth in abundant loyalty and love towards all men in common. For this gift, through the knowledge of truth which is imparted to us in its light, establishes in us a wide-stretching love toward all in common. Now the most simple are also the most tranquil, and have the most peace in themselves; and are the most deeply immersed in God; and are most enlightened in understanding, and most fruitful in good works, and in outflowing love toward all in common. And they are hindered least, for they are most like unto God; for God is simplicity in His Being, clarity in His understanding, and outflowing and universal love in His works. And the more we are like unto God in these three things, so much the more closely are we united with Him. And for this reason we must remain simple in our ground, and must apprehend all things by means of enlightened reason, and must flow forth through all things in universal love. So likewise the sun in the heavens, though it abides in itself simple and unchanged, sends forth its light and heat to the whole world in common.

Now understand how we should live with enlightened reason in universal love. The Father is the Origin of the whole Godhead according to Essence and according to Personality. We therefore should bow down in spirit, in humble awe, before the sublimity of the Father : and thereby we possess humility, the foundation of all the virtues. We should fervently adore, that is to say, we should honour and reverence, the mightiness of the Father, because He, in His might, creates and preserves all things out of nothing. And thereby we shall be lifted up in ghostly wise. We should offer praise and thanks and everlasting service to the faithfulness and love of God, Who has freed us from the fetters of the enemy and from eternal death : and thereby we shall be made free. We should present and bewail before the wisdom of God the blindness and ignorance of human nature ; and should crave that all men may become enlightened, and may attain to the knowledge of truth : thus God shall be known and honoured by them. We should pray for the mercy of God upon sinners, that thus they may be converted, and may grow in virtue : thus God shall be loved by them with a desirous love. We should give generously to all those who have need of it of the rich treasures of God, that therewith they may all be filled, and may flow back towards God :

and thus God shall be possessed by them all. We
should offer to the Father, with awe and reverence,
all the service and all the works which Christ, according to His manhood, fulfilled in love : thus all our
prayers shall be heard. We should also offer to the
Father in Christ Jesus all the fervent devotion of the
angels and the saints and the just : so we shall be
united with them all in the glory of God. We should
also offer up to the Father the whole service of Holy
Church, and the Holy Sacrifice of all the priests, and
all that we may achieve and think, in the name of
Christ; that thereby we may go out to meet God
through Christ, and may become like unto Him in
universal love, and may transcend all likeness in
simplicity, and may be united with Him within the
Essential Unity. We should ever abide in oneness
with God, and should eternally flow forth with God
and all His saints in universal love, and continually
return with thankfulness and praise, and immerse
ourselves in fruitive love in the Essential Rest. This
is the richest life of which I know : and in it we possess
the gift of Understanding.

The Gift of Wisdom

Now understand this well : when we turn within
ourselves in contemplation, the fruitive unity of God
is like to a darkness, a somewhat which is unconditioned and incomprehensible. And the spirit turns
inward through love and through simplicity of intention, because it is active in all virtues, offering itself
up in fruition above all virtues. In this loving introversion, there arises the seventh gift, which is the
spirit of Savouring Wisdom;   and it saturates the

simplicity of our spirit, soul and body, with wisdom and with ghostly savours. And it is a ghostly touch or stirring within the unity of our spirit ; and it is an inpouring and a source of all grace, all gifts and all virtues. And, in this touch of God, each man savours his exercise and his life according to the power of the touch and the measure of his love. And this Divine stirring is the inmost mediator between God and ourselves, between rest and activity, between the conditioned and the unconditioned, between eternity and time. And God works this ghostly touching within us first of all, before all gifts ; and yet it is known and tasted by us last of all. For only when we have lovingly sought God in all our practices even to the inward deeps of our ground, do we first feel the gushing in of all the graces and gifts of God ; and we feel this touch in the unity of our highest powers, above reason, but not without reason, for we understand in truth that we are touched. But if we would know what this is and whence it comes, then reason and all creaturely observation fail. For though the air be illuminated by the sunlight, and the eyes be sharp and sound, if one would follow the rays which bring the brightness, and look at the disc of the sun, the eyes would fail in their activity, and would only receive the lustre of the rays in a passive way. So likewise, the reflection of the Incomprehensible Light in the unity of our highest power is so intense that all creaturely activity which works in distinction must fail. And here our activity must passively endure the interior working of God, which is the source of all Divine gifts. For could we receive God Himself into our comprehension, He would give Himself to us without intermediary ; but this is impossible to us because we are too narrow and too little to comprehend God. And therefore He pours His gifts into us according to the measure of our comprehension and the worthiness of our practices. For the fruitful unity of God ever abides above the unity of our powers and ever demands of us likeness in love and in virtues. And that is why we are touched again and again, that we may each time be renewed and become more like Him in the virtues. And, through these renewed touches, the spirit falls into hunger and thirst, and would taste through and through, and pass through and through the whole abyss in a storm of love, that thereby it may be satisfied. Hence there comes an eternal, hungry craving, and an eternal unsatisfied desire. For all loving spirits desire and strive after God, each according to its nobleness and the measure in which it has been touched by God; yet God remains eternally incomprehensible by way of our active desires, and therefore there abides in us, together with all saints, an eternal hunger, and an eternal desirous introversion. And in the meeting with God, the radiance and the heat are so great and so limitless that all spirits must fail in their activity, and must melt and vanish away in sensible love in the unity of their spirit. And here they must passively endure as sheer creatures the working of God. And here our spirit and Divine grace and all our virtues are one sensible love without activity; for our spirit has spent itself and has itself become love. And here the spirit is simple and susceptible of all gifts and is capable of every virtue. And, in this ground of sensible love, there dwells the gushing spring, that is, the inpouring or inward working of God, which at every hour moves us and urges us and draws us inward and causes us to flow forth into new works of virtue. Thus I have shown to you the ground and the condition of all the virtues.

CHAPTER LXIV

OF THE HIGHEST DEGREE OF THE MOST INTERIOR LIFE

Now understand this well : that measureless Splendour of God, which together with the incomprehensible brightness, is the cause of all gifts and of all virtues—that same Uncomprehended Light transfigures the fruitive tendency of our spirit and penetrates it in a way that is wayless ; that is, through the Uncomprehended Light. And in this light the spirit immerses itself in fruitive rest ; for this rest is wayless and fathomless, and one can know of it in no other way than through itself—that is, through rest. For, could we know and comprehend it, it would fall into mode and measure ; then it could not satisfy us, but rest would become an eternal restlessness. And for this reason, the simple, loving and immersed tendency of our spirit works within us a fruitive love ; and this fruitive love is abysmal. And the abyss of God calls to the abyss ; that is, of all those who are united with the Spirit of God in fruitive love. This inward call is an inundation of the essential brightness, and this essential brightness, enfolding us in an abysmal love, causes us to be lost to ourselves, and to flow forth from ourselves into the wild darkness of the Godhead. And, thus united without means, and made one with the Spirit of God, we can meet God through God, and everlastingly possess with Him and in Him our eternal bliss.

CHAPTER LXV

OF THREE KINDS OF MOST INWARD PRACTICES

This most inward life is practised in three ways.

At times, the inward man performs his introspection simply, according to the fruitive tendency, above all activity and above all virtues, through a simple inward gazing in the fruition of love. And here he meets God without intermediary. And from out the Divine Unity, there shines into him a simple light; and this light shows him Darkness and Nakedness and Nothingness. In the Darkness, he is enwrapped and falls into somewhat which is in no wise, even as one who has lost his way. In the Nakedness, he loses the perception and discernment of all things, and is transfigured and penetrated by a simple light. In the Nothingness, all his activity fails him; for he is vanquished by the working of God's abysmal love, and in the fruitive inclination of his spirit he vanquishes God, and becomes one spirit with him. And in this oneness with the Spirit of God, he enters into a fruitive tasting and possesses the Being of God. And he is filled, according to the measure in which he has sunk himself in his essential being, with the abysmal delights and riches of God. And from these riches an envelopment and a plenitude of sensible love flow forth into the unity of the higher powers. And from this plenitude of sensible love, a savoury and penetrating satisfaction flows forth into the heart and the bodily powers. And through this inflow the man becomes immovable within, and helpless as regards himself and all his works. And in the deeps of his ground he knows and feels nothing, in soul or in body, but a singular radiance with a sensible well-being and an all-pervading savour. This is the first way, and it is the way of emptiness; for it makes a man empty of all things, and lifts him up above activity and above all the virtues. And it unites the man with God, and brings about a firm perseverance in the most interior practices which he can cultivate. When, however, any restlessness, or working of the virtues, puts intermediaries, or images, between the inward man and the naked introversion which he desires, then he is hindered in this exercise; for this way consists in a going out, beyond all things, into the Emptiness. This is the first form of the most inward exercise.

. . . . . .

At times such an inward man turns towards God with ardent desire and activity; that he may glorify and honour Him, and offer up and annihilate in the love of God, his selfhood and all that he is able to do. And here he meets God through an intermediary. This intermediary is the gift of Savouring Wisdom, the ground and origin of all virtues; which enkindles and moves all good men according to the measure of their love, and at times so greatly stirs and enkindles the inward man through love, that all the gifts of God, and all that God may give, except the gift of Himself, seem too little to him, and cannot satisfy him, but rather increase his impatience. For he has an inward perception or feeling in his ground; where all the virtues begin and end, where love dwells, and where with ardent desire he offers up all his virtues to God. And here the hunger and thirst of love become so great that he perpetually surrenders himself, and gives up his own works, and empties

himself, and is noughted in love, for he is hungry and
thirsty for the taste of God ; and, at each irradiation
of God,   he is seized by God, and more than ever
before is newly touched by love. Living he dies, and
dying he lives again. And in this way the desirous
hunger and thirst of love are renewed in him every
hour.

This is the second way, which is the way of longing,
in which love dwells in the Divine likeness, and longs
and craves to unite itself with God. This way is more
profitable and honourable to us than the first, for it is
the source of the first ; for none can enter into the
rest which is above all works save the man who has
loved love with desire and with activity. And this
is why the grace of God and our active love must both
go before and follow after ; that is to say, they must
be practised both before and after. For without acts
of love we cannot merit anything, neither achieve
God, nor keep the possession of that which we have
acquired through the works of love. And for this
reason no one who has power over himself, and can
practise love, should be idle. When, however, a
good man lingers in any gift of God, or any creature,
he will be hindered in this most inward exercise ; for
this exercise is a hunger which nothing can still, save
God alone.

.   .   .   .   .   .

From these two ways the third way arises ; and
this is an inward life according to justice. Now
understand this : God comes to us without ceasing,
both with means and without means, and demands
of us both action and fruition, in such a way that the
one never impedes, but always strengthens, the other.
And therefore the most inward man lives his life in

these two ways : namely, in work and in rest.

And in each he is whole and undivided ; for he is wholly in God because he rests in fruition, and he is wholly in himself because he loves in activity : and he is perpetually called and urged by God to renew both the rest and the work. And the justice of the spirit desires to pay every hour that which is demanded of it by God. And therefore, at each irradiation of God, the spirit turns inward, in action and in fruition ; and thus it is renewed in every virtue, and is more deeply immersed in fruitive rest. For God gives, in one gift, Himself and His gifts ; and the spirit gives, at each introversion, itself and all its works. For by means of the simple irradiation of God and the fruitive tendency and melting away of love, the spirit has been united with God, and is incessantly transported into rest. And through the gifts of Understanding and Savouring Wisdom, it is touched in an active way, and perpetually enlightened and enkindled in love. And there is shown and presented to it in the spirit all that one may desire. It is hungry and thirsty, for it beholds the food of the angels and the heavenly drink. It works diligently in love, for it beholds its rest. It is a pilgrim ; and it sees its country. In love it strives for victory ; for it sees its crown. Consolation, peace, joy, beauty and riches, and all that can delight it, are shown without measure in ghostly images to the reason which is enlightened in God. And through this showing and the touch of God, love remains active. For this just man has established a true life in the spirit, in rest and in work, which shall endure eternally ; but, after this life, it shall be changed into a higher state. Thus the man is just ; and he

goes *towards* God with fervent love in eternal activity ;
and he goes *in* God with fruitive inclination in eternal
rest.   And he dwells in God, and yet goes forth towards all creatures in universal love, in virtue, and
in justice.   And this is the supreme summit of the
inward life.   All those men who do not possess both
rest and work in one and the same exercise, have
not yet attained this justice.   This just man cannot
be hindered in his introversion, for he turns inward
both in fruition and in work ; but he is like to a double
mirror, which receives images on both sides.   For
in his higher part, the man receives God with all His
gifts ; and, in his lower part, he receives bodily images
through the senses.   Now he can enter into himself
at will, and can practise justice without hindrance.
But man is unstable in this life, and that is why he
often turns outwards, and works in the senses, without need and without the command of the enlightened
reason ; and thus he falls into venial sins.   But in
the loving introversion of the just man all venial sins
are like to drops of water in a glowing furnace.

And with this I leave the inward life.

CHAPTER LXVI

SHOWING HOW SOME MEN LIVE CONTRARY TO THESE EXERCISES

Now some men, who seem to be righteous, yet live
contrary to these three ways and to every virtue.
Let every one observe and prove himself ! Every
man who is not drawn and enlightened of God is not
touched by love, and has neither the active cleaving

with desire   nor the simple and loving tendency
to fruitive rest. And therefore such a one cannot
unite himself with God; for all those who live
without supernatural love are inclined towards themselves and seek their rest in outward things. For all
creatures by their nature tend towards rest : and
therefore, rest is sought both by the good and by the
evil, in divers ways.

Now mark this : when a man is bare and imageless in his senses, and empty and idle in his higher
powers (30), he enters into rest through mere nature ;
and this rest may be found and possessed within themselves in mere nature by all creatures, without the
grace of God, whenever they can strip themselves of
images and of all activity. But in this the loving man
cannot find his rest, for charity and the inward touch
of God's grace will not be still : and so the inward
man cannot long remain in natural rest within himself.

But now mark the way in which this natural rest
is practised. It is a sitting still, without either outward or inward acts, in vacancy, in order that rest
may be found and may remain untroubled. But a
rest which is practised in this way is unlawful ; for
it brings with it in men a blindness and ignorance,
and a sinking down into themselves without activity.
Such a rest is nought else than an idleness, into
which the man has fallen, and in which he forgets
himself and God and all things in all that has to do
with activity. This rest is wholly contrary to the
supernatural rest, which one possesses in God ; for
that is a loving self-mergence joined to a simple
gazing into the Incomprehensible Brightness. This
rest in God, which is actively sought with inward
longing, and is found in fruitive inclination, and is

eternally possessed in the self-mergence of love, and which, when possessed, is sought none the less : this rest is exalted above the rest of mere nature as greatly as God is exalted above all creatures. And that is why all those men are deceived who have self in mind and sink down in the natural rest, and neither seek God in desire, nor find Him in fruitive love ; for the rest which they find consists in their own idleness, to which they are inclined by nature and by habit. And in this natural rest one cannot find God, but it certainly leads a man into a bare vacancy, which may be found by Pagans and Jews and all men, how wicked soever they may be, if they can live in their sins without the reproach of their conscience, and can empty themselves of every image and of all activity. In this bare vacancy the rest is pleasant and great. This rest is in itself no sin ; for it exists in all men by nature, whenever they make themselves empty. But when a man wishes to practise and possess it without acts of virtue, he falls into spiritual pride and a self-complacency, from which he seldom recovers. And he sometimes fancies himself to have and to be that to which he shall never attain. When a man thus possesses this rest in false quietude, and all loving adherence seems a hindrance to him, he clings to himself in his rest, and lives contrary to the first way in which man is united with God : and this is the beginning of all ghostly error.

Now consider a similitude of this : the angels who turned inward towards God in love and fruition, with all that they had received from Him, found beatitude and eternal rest ; but those who turned towards themselves, and sought rest in themselves with self-complacency in the natural light, their rest was short and was unlawful. And they were blinded, and there was a wall of separation between them and the eternal light, and they fell into darkness and eternal restlessness. This is the first contrary way; which one possesses by resting in false quietude.

.   .   .   .   .   .

Now mark this: when a man wishes to possess inward rest in idleness, without inward and desirous cleaving to God, then he is ready for all errors; for he is turned away from God, and inclined towards himself, in natural love, seeking and desiring consolation and sweetness and everything that pleases him. And such a man is like to a merchant, for in all his activity he is turned only towards himself, and seeks and means his own rest and his own profit, more than the glory of God. A man who thus lives in mere natural love, always possesses himself in self-love without self-renunciation. Such men often lead a hard life with great works of penitence, that they may become known and renowned for their great sanctity, and also that they may merit a great reward; for all natural love is favourably disposed to itself and likes to receive great honours in time and a great reward in eternity. And these men have many special desires, and pray and beseech God for many particular things. And thus they are often deceived; for sometimes, through the work of the devil, those things which they desire happen to them, and then they ascribe this to their sanctity, and hold themselves worthy of them all; for such people are proud, and neither touched nor enlightened by God. And therefore they dwell within themselves, and a small consolation may greatly rejoice them, for they know not what they lack. And they are wholly attached, in their desire, to inward savours and the spiritual refreshment of their nature. And this is called spiritual lust; for it is an inordinate attachment in natural love, which is always directed towards itself, and seeks its own profit in all things.

Such men are always spiritually proud and self-willed; and this is why their desires and lusts are sometimes so vehemently set upon the things which they desire, and wilfully strive to acquire from God, so that they are often deceived, and some of them also become possessed by the devil. All these men live contrary to charity and to the loving introversion in which a man offers himself up, with all that he can achieve, for the honour and love of God; and in which nothing can give him rest or satisfaction but a single incomprehensible Good, which is God alone. For charity is a bond of love, in which we are drawn up to God, and through which we renounce ourselves, and whereby we are united with God and God is united with us. But natural love turns back towards itself, and towards its own profit, and ever abides alone. Nevertheless, in its outward works, natural love is as like unto charity as two hairs from the same head; but the intentions are different. For the good man always seeks and means and desires, with an aspiring heart (27), to glorify God; but in natural love a man has always himself and his own profit in mind. Therefore, when natural love opposes and conquers true charity, the man falls into four sins; namely, spiritual pride, avarice, gluttony, and lust. And in this way Adam fell in Paradise, and all human nature with him; for he loved himself inordinately with natural love, and so he turned away from God, and scorned in his pride the commandment of God. And he desired knowledge and wisdom in his avarice; and he sought pleasant tastes and satisfactions in gluttony; and after that he was moved by lust. But Mary was a living Paradise. She found the grace which Adam lost, and much more besides, for she is the Mother of Love. She turned in active charity towards God, and conceived Christ in humility. And she offered Him up to the Father with all His sufferings in generosity; and she never tasted of consolation, nor of any gift, in gluttony; and her whole life was in purity. Whosoever follows her shall conquer all that is contrary to the virtues, and shall enter into the kingdom where she reigns with her Son in eternity.

.   .   .   .   .   .

So, when a man possesses the natural rest in bare vacancy, whilst in all his works he has himself in mind, and he continues obstinately disobedient in his self-will, he cannot be united with God; for he lives without charity in unlikeness to God. And here begins the third contrary way, which is the most noxious of all; and this is an unrighteous life, full of ghostly error and of all perversity.

Now mark well what follows, lest you should not understand it well. All these men are, in their own opinion, God-seeing men, and believe themselves the holiest of all men living. Yet they live contrary and unlike to God and all saints and all good men. Observe the following marks: thus you will be able to recognise them both by their words and their works. By means of the natural rest which they feel and possess in themselves in bare vacancy, they believe themselves to be free, and to be united with God without means, and to be above all the customs of Holy Church, and above the commandments of God, and above the law, and above every work of virtue which can in any way be done. For they think their idleness to be so great a thing that it may not be troubled by any work, how good soever it be ; for this idleness is nobler than any virtue. And therefore they maintain themselves in pure passivity, without any activity towards above or towards below; like a loom, which does not work of itself, but awaits its master, and the time when he wishes to work. For they deem that if they worked themselves, God would be hindered in His work. And therefore they are empty of every virtue ; and indeed so empty, that they will neither praise nor thank God. They have no knowledge and no love, no will, no prayer, no desire ; for they believe that all that they could pray for, and desire, is already possessed of them. And so they are poor of spirit, for they are without will, and have forsaken everything, and live without any personal preferences : and thus it seems to them that they are empty, and have overcome everything, and have in their possession all those things for which the customs of Holy Church have been instituted and ordained. And so, they say, no one, not even God, can give them anything, or can take away anything from them ; for they have, in their own opinion, transcended all customs and all virtues, and have entered into the pure emptiness, and are released from every virtue. And this release from all virtues in emptiness needs, they say, more labour than the acquisition of the virtues. And therefore they would be free, and obedient to none ; neither pope, nor bishop, nor parson. Even though outwardly they seem to be so, inwardly they are submissive to none, neither in will nor in works ; for they are in every respect empty of all that Holy

Church practises. And therefore they say, as long as a man strives after virtue, and desires to fulfil the good pleasure of God, he is still imperfect ; for he is still amassing virtues, and knows not this spiritual poverty and emptiness. But they are themselves, in their own opinion, lifted up above all the choirs of saints and angels, and above every reward which one can in any way merit. And therefore they say that their virtues can nevermore increase, nor can they themselves deserve a greater reward, nor commit any sin any more; for, they say, they live without will, and have surrendered their spirit to God in rest and bareness, and are one with God, and in themselves have become nothing And therefore they can do without hindrance all that the bodily nature desires, for they have attained to the state of innocence, and no law has sway over them. When therefore it happens that their emptiness of spirit is troubled or hindered by any natural lust, they yield to nature, that their emptiness of spirit may remain untroubled. And that is why they do not keep Lent or Ember-days, or any other commandment, save when they do it for the sake of their neighbours ; for they live without conscience in all things. I hope that of such folk not many are to be found ; but those who are like them are the most wicked and vile of all men living. And they are sometimes possessed of the Fiend ; and then they are so cunning that one cannot vanquish them on the grounds of reason. But through Holy Scripture and the teaching of Christ and our Faith, we may prove that they are deceived.

CHAPTER LXVII

OF ANOTHER KIND OF PERVERTED MEN

Now we find yet another kind of perverted men, who are in some points different from those already described ; though they too believe themselves to be exempted from all works, and to be instruments with which God works what He wills. And therefore they say that they are in a purely passive state without activity ; and that the works which God works through them are noble and meritorious beyond anything that another man, working his works himself by the grace of God, could do. And therefore they say that they are God-passive men,   and that they do nothing of themselves, but that God works all their works. And they say they can do no sin : for it is God Who does all their works, and in themselves they are empty of all things. And all that God wills is worked through them, and nothing else. These men have surrendered themselves to inward passivity in their emptiness ; and live without preference for any one thing. And they have a resigned and humble appearance, and can very well endure and suffer with equanimity all that befalls them ; for they hold themselves to be the instruments with which God works according to His will. Such men in many of their ways and works are like in their conduct to good men, but in some things they differ from them ; for all things to which they are inwardly urged, whether these be virtuous or not, they believe to proceed from the Holy Ghost. And in this and in suchlike things, they are deceived ; for the Spirit of God neither wills, counsels, nor works, in any man things which are contrary to the teaching of Christ and Holy Christianity.

Such folk are hard to recognise, save by the man who is enlightened, and has received the power of discerning spirits and divine truth ; for many amongst them are cunning in outward things and know well how to cloak and make fair their perversity. And they are so self-willed, and hold so fast to their own peculiar ideas, that they would sooner die than abandon one point of the thing they have laid hold on ; for they hold themselves the holiest and most enlightened of all men living.

These men differ from the first kind in this, that they say that they can grow and acquire merit : whereas the others hold that they cannot merit anything more, for they possess themselves in unity and emptiness, wherefrom one cannot rise higher, because here there is no more activity. These are all perverted men, and are the most wicked of the living ; and they are to be abhorred as if they were the Fiend in hell. But if you have well understood that teaching which I have given you heretofore in various ways, you will perceive that these men are deceived. For they live contrary to God and righteousness and all saints ; and they are all precursors of the Antichrist, preparing his way in every unbelief. For they would be free, without the commandments of God, and without virtues ; and empty and united with God, without love and charity. And they would be God-seeing men without loving and steadfast contemplation, and the holiest of all men living without the works of holiness. And they say that they rest in Him Whom they do not love ; and are uplifted into That which they neither will nor desire. And they say that they are stripped of every virtue, and of diligent devotion to God, lest they should hinder God in His working. They confess, indeed, that God is the Creator and Lord over all creatures, and yet they will neither thank nor praise Him. They confess that His power and His riches are without end, and yet they say that He can neither give nor take from them anything, neither can they grow nor acquire merit.

And sometimes too they uphold the opposite, and say that they merit a greater wage than other men ; for God does their works, and they themselves endure passively the workings of God, without co-operation, since these are worked of Him. And in this, they say, lies the supreme merit. But this is altogether illusion and impossibility. For the activity of God is in itself eternal and unchangeable ; for He is His own activity and nought else. And in this working there can be no growth, nor merit of any creature whatsoever ; for here there is nothing but God, Who can neither wax nor wane. But the creatures, by virtue of God, have their own activity, in nature and in grace, and also in glory : and if their works end in grace here, they shall continue in glory for ever. Now were it possible, which it is not, that a spiritual creature could be annihilated as regards its activity, and thereby became even as empty as it was when it was not made—that is, that it could become wholly one with God, as it was then—it could acquire no merit, no more than it could before creation. Further, it would be neither holier nor more blessed than a stone or a log of wood ; for without our own work and the knowledge and love of God, we cannot be blessed. Though God would indeed be blessed, as He is eternally, yet it would not avail us. And therefore

that which these say of their emptiness is all deceit ;
for they wish to excuse all wickedness and perversity,
and give these out as nobler and more sublime than
all the virtues. And they would cunningly disguise
the worst, so that it should seem the best. All these
are contrary to God and all His saints ; but they have
a likeness to the damned spirits in hell, for these too
are without charity and without knowledge, and are
empty of thanksgivings and praise and of all loving
adherence ; and this is the cause, why they remain
damned in eternity. And that these folk may be like
to them, they lack only this, that they should fall
from time into eternity, and that the justice of God
be revealed in their works.

But Christ the Son of God, Who according to His
manhood is the pattern and the head of all good men,
showing them how to live, He was and is and everlastingly shall abide with all His members, that is,
with all His saints, in love and longing, thankfulness
and praise, toward His heavenly Father. Nevertheless, His soul was and is united with the Divine
Essence and blessed therein. But to this bare idleness He never could, nor ever shall, come ; for His
glorified soul, and all who are blessed, have an eternal
loving striving, even as those who have tasted of God,
and are hungry and thirsty, and can nevermore be
satisfied. Yet that very soul of Christ, and all saints,
partake of God above all desires, where there is nothing
but the One. This is the eternal bliss of God and of
all His chosen. And that is why fruition and activity
are the blessedness of Christ and all His saints ; and
this is the life of all good men, each according to the
measure of his love. And this is a righteousness
that shall never pass away. And that is why we

should adorn ourselves, from without and from within, with virtues and with goodly behaviour, as do the saints ; and should lovingly and humbly exercise ourselves before the eyes of God in all our works.   Then we shall meet God by means of all His gifts.   And then we shall be touched by sensible love, and shall be filled with loyalty towards all.   And so we shall flow forth and flow back again in true charity, and shall be firmly established and steadfast within ourselves in simple peace and in the Divine likeness.   And by means of this likeness and fruitive love and the Divine brightness, we shall be melted into the unity, and shall meet God through God, without means, in fruitive rest.   And so we shall eternally remain within, and yet continually flow forth and incessantly flow back again.   And herewith we shall possess a veritable inward life in all perfection,   That this may come to pass in us, so help us God.   AMEN.

THE END OF THE SECOND BOOK

HERE BEGINS

THE THIRD BOOK

CHAPTER I

SHOWING THE THREE WAYS BY WHICH ONE ENTERS INTO THE GOD-SEEING LIFE

THE inward lover of God, who possesses God in fruitive love, and himself in adhering and active love, and his whole life in virtues according to righteousness; through these three things, and by the mysterious revelation of God, such an inward man enters into the God-seeing life. Yea, the lover who is inward and righteous, him will it please God in His freedom to choose and to lift up into a superessential contemplation, in the Divine Light and according to the Divine Way. This contemplation sets us in purity and clearness above all our understanding, for it is a singular adornment and a heavenly crown, and besides the eternal reward of all virtues and of our whole life. And to it none can attain through knowledge and subtlety, neither through any exercise whatsoever. Only he with whom it pleases God to be united in His Spirit, and whom it pleases Him to enlighten by Himself, can see God, and no one else. The mysterious Divine Nature is eternally and actively beholding and loving according to the Persons, and has everlasting fruition in a mutual embrace of the Persons

167

in the unity of the Essence. In this embrace, in the essential Unity of God, all inward spirits are one with God in the immersion of love ; and are that same one which the Essence is in Itself, according to the mode of Eternal Bliss. And in this most high unity of the Divine Nature, the heavenly Father is origin and beginning of every work which is worked in heaven and on earth. And He says in the deep-sunken hiddenness of the spirit : BEHOLD, THE BRIDE-GROOM COMETH ; GO YE OUT TO MEET HIM.

These words we will now explain and set forth in their relation to that superessential contemplation which is the source of all holiness, and of all perfection of life to which one may attain. Few men can attain to this Divine seeing, because of their own incapacity and the mysteriousness of the light in which one sees. And therefore no one will thoroughly understand the meaning of it by any learning or subtle consideration of his own ; for all words, and all that may be learnt and understood in a creaturely way, are foreign to, and far below, the truth which I mean. But he who is united with God, and is enlightened in this truth, he is able to understand the truth by itself. For to comprehend and to understand God above all similitudes, such as He is in Himself, is to be God with God, without intermediary, and without any otherness that can become a hindrance or an intermediary. And therefore I beg every one who cannot understand this, or feel it in the fruitive unity of his spirit, that he be not offended at it, and leave it for that which it is : for that which I am going to say is true, and Christ, the Eternal Truth, has said it Himself in His teaching in many places, if we could but show and explain it rightly. And therefore, whosoever wishes to understand this must have died to himself, and must live in God, and must turn his gaze to the eternal light in the ground of his spirit, where the Hidden Truth reveals Itself without means. For our Heavenly Father wills that we should see ; for He is the Father of Light, and this is why He utters eternally, without intermediary and without interruption, in the hiddenness of our spirit, one unique and abysmal word, and no other. And in this word, He utters Himself and all things. And this word is none other than : BEHOLD. And this is the coming forth and the birth of the Son of Eternal Light, in Whom all blessedness is known and seen.

. . . . . .

Now if the spirit would see God with God in this Divine light without means, there needs must be on the part of man three things.

The first is that he must be perfectly ordered from without in all the virtues, and within must be unencumbered, and as empty of every outward work as if he did not work at all : for if his emptiness is troubled within by some work of virtue, he has an image ; and as long as this endures within him, he cannot contemplate.

Secondly, he must inwardly cleave to God, with adhering intention and love, even as a burning and glowing fire which can never more be quenched. As long as he feels himself to be in this state, he is able to contemplate.

Thirdly, he must have lost himself in a Waylessness and in a Darkness, in which all contemplative men wander in fruition and wherein they never again can find themselves in a creaturely way. In the abyss of this darkness, in which the loving spirit has died to

itself, there begin the manifestation of God and eternal life. For in this darkness there shines and is born an incomprehensible Light, which is the Son of God, in Whom we behold eternal life. And in this Light one becomes seeing ; and this Divine Light is given to the simple sight of the spirit, where the spirit receives the brightness which is God Himself, above all gifts and every creaturely activity, in the idle emptiness in which the spirit has lost itself through fruitive love, and where it receives without means the brightness of God, and is changed without interruption into that brightness which it receives. Behold, this mysterious brightness, in which one sees everything that one can desire according to the emptiness of the spirit : this brightness is so great that the loving contemplative, in his ground wherein he rests, sees and feels nothing but an incomprehensible Light ; and through that Simple Nudity which enfolds all things, he finds himself, and feels himself, to be that same Light by which he sees, and nothing else.
And this is the first condition by which one becomes seeing in the Divine Light. Blessed are the eyes which are thus seeing, for they possess eternal life.

CHAPTER II

HOW THE ETERNAL BIRTH OF GOD IS RENEWED WITHOUT INTERRUPTION IN THE NOBILITY OF THE SPIRIT

WHEN we have thus become seeing, we can behold in joy the eternal coming of our Bridegroom ; and that is the second point of which we would speak. What is this coming of our Bridegroom which is eternal ?

It is the new birth and a new enlightenment without interruption ; for the ground from which the Light shines forth, and which is the Light itself, is life-giving and fruitful, and therefore the manifestation of the Eternal Light is renewed without ceasing in the hiddenness of the spirit. Behold, every creaturely work, and every exercise of virtue, must here cease ; for here God works alone in the high nobility of the spirit. And here there is nothing but an eternal seeing and staring at that Light, by that Light, and in that Light. And the coming of the Bridegroom is so swift that He is perpetually coming, and yet dwelling within with unfathomable riches ; and ever coming anew, in His Person, without interruption, with such new brightness that it seems as though he had never come before. For His coming consists, beyond time, in an eternal NOW, which is ever received with new longings and new joy. Behold, the delight and the joy which this Bridegroom brings with Him in His coming are boundless and without measure, for they are Himself. And this is why the eyes with which the spirit sees and gazes at its Bridegroom, have opened so wide that they can never close again. For the spirit continues for ever to see and to stare at the secret manifestation of God. And the grasp of the spirit is opened so wide for the coming in of the Bridegroom, that the spirit itself becomes that Breadth Which it grasps. And so God is grasped and beheld through God ; wherein rests all our blessedness. This is the second point : in which we receive, without interruption, the eternal coming of our Bridegroom in our spirit.

CHAPTER III

HOW OUR SPIRIT IS CALLED TO GO OUT IN CONTEMPLATION AND FRUITION

Now the Spirit of God says in the secret outpouring of our spirit : Go ye out, in an eternal contemplation and fruition, according to the way of God. All the riches which are in God by nature we possess by way of love in God, and God in us, through the un- measured love which is the Holy Ghost ; for in this love one tastes of all that one can desire. And there- fore through this love we are dead to ourselves, and have gone forth in loving immersion into Wayless- ness and Darkness. There the spirit is embraced by the Holy Trinity, and dwells for ever within the superessential Unity, in rest and fruition. And in that same Unity, according to Its fruitfulness, the Father dwells in the Son, and the Son in the Father, and all creatures dwell in Both. And this is above the distinction of the Persons ; for here by means of the reason we understand Fatherhood and Sonhood as the life-giving fruitfulness of the Divine Nature.

Here there arise and begin an eternal going out and an eternal work which is without beginning ; for here there is a beginning with beginning. For, after the Almighty Father had perfectly comprehended Him- self in the ground of His fruitfulness, so the Son, the Eternal Word of the Father, came forth as the second Person in the Godhead. And, through the Eternal Birth, all creatures have come forth in eternity, before they were created in time. So God has seen and known them in Himself, according to distinction, in living ideas,   and in an otherness from Himself ;

but not as something other in all ways, for all that is in God is God. This eternal going out and this eternal life, which we have and are in God eternally, without ourselves, is the cause of our created being in time. And our created being abides in the Eternal Essence, and is one with it in its essential existence. And this eternal life and being, which we have and are in the eternal Wisdom of God, is like unto God. For it has an eternal immanence in the Divine Essence, without distinction; and through the birth of the Son it has an eternal outflowing in a distinction and otherness, according to the Eternal Idea. And through these two points it is so like unto God that He knows and reflects Himself in this likeness without cessation, according to the Essence and according to the Persons. For, though even here there are distinction and otherness according to intellectual perception, yet this likeness is one with that same Image of the Holy Trinity, which is the wisdom of God and in which God beholds Himself and all things in an eternal Now, without before and after. In a single seeing He beholds Himself and all things. And this is the Image and the Likeness of God, and our Image and our Likeness; for in it God reflects Himself and all things. In this Divine Image all creatures have an eternal life, outside themselves, as in their eternal Archetype; and after this eternal Image, and in this Likeness, we have been made by the Holy Trinity. And therefore God wills that we shall go forth from ourselves in this Divine Light, and shall reunite ourselves in a supernatural way with this Image, which is our proper life, and shall possess it with Him, in action and in fruition, in eternal bliss.

For we know well that the bosom of the Father is

our ground and origin, in which we begin our being
and our life. And from our proper ground, that is
from the Father and from all that lives in Him,
there shines forth an eternal brightness, which is
the birth of the Son. And in this brightness, that
is, in the Son, the Father knows Himself and all that
lives in Him ; for all that He has, and all that He is,
He gives to the Son, save only the property of Fatherhood, which abides in Himself. And this is why
all that lives in the Father, unmanifested in the
Unity, is also in the Son actively poured forth into
manifestation : and the simple ground of our Eternal
Image ever remains in darkness and in waylessness,
but the brightness without limit which streams forth
from it, this reveals and brings forth within the
Conditioned the hiddenness of God. And all those
men who are raised up above their created being into
a God-seeing life are one with this Divine brightness.
And they are that brightness itself, and they see,
feel, and find, even by means of this Divine Light, that,
as regards their uncreated essence, they are that
same onefold ground from which the brightness without limit shines forth in the Divine way, and which,
according to the simplicity of the Essence, abides eternally onefold and wayless within. And this is why
inward and God-seeing men will go out in the way of
contemplation, above reason and above distinction
and above their created being, through an eternal
intuitive gazing. By means of this inborn light they
are transfigured, and made one with that same light
through which they see and which they see. And
thus the God-seeing men follow after their Eternal
Image, after which they have been made ; and they
behold God and all things, without distinction, in a

simple seeing, in the Divine brightness. And this
is the most noble and the most profitable contemplation to which one can attain in this life; for in
this contemplation, a man best remains master of
himself and free. And at each loving introversion he
may grow in nobility of life beyond anything that
we are able to understand; for he remains free and
master of himself in inwardness and virtue. And
this gazing at the Divine Light holds him up above all
inwardness and all virtue and all merit, for it is the
crown and the reward after which we strive, and
which we have and possess now in this wise; for
a God-seeing life is a heavenly life. But were we
set free from this misery and this exile, so we should
have, as regards our created being, a greater capacity
to receive this brightness; and so the glory of God
would shine through us in every way better and more
nobly. This is the way above all ways, in which
one goes out through Divine contemplation and an
eternal intuitive gazing, and in which one is transfigured and transmuted in the Divine brightness.
This going out of the God-seeing man is also in love;
for through the fruition of love he rises above his
created being, and finds and tastes the riches and the
delights which are God Himself, and which He causes
to pour forth without interruption in the hiddenness
of the spirit, where the spirit is like unto the nobility
of God.

CHAPTER IV

OF A DIVINE MEETING WHICH TAKES PLACE IN THE HIDDENNESS OF OUR SPIRIT

WHEN the inward and God-seeing man has thus attained to his Eternal Image, and in this clearness, through the Son, has entered into the bosom of the Father : then he is enlightened by Divine truth, and he receives anew, every moment, the Eternal Birth, and he goes forth according to the way of the light, in a Divine contemplation. And here there begins the fourth and last point ; namely, a loving meeting, in which, above all else, our highest blessedness consists.

You should know that the heavenly Father, as a living ground, with all that lives in Him, is actively turned towards His Son, as to His own Eternal Wisdom. And that same Wisdom, with all that lives in It, is actively turned back towards the Father, that is, towards that very ground from which It comes forth. And in this meeting, there comes forth the third Person, between the Father and the Son ; that is the Holy Ghost, Their mutual Love, who is one with them Both in the same nature. And He enfolds and drenches through both in action and fruition the Father and the Son, and all that lives in Both, with such great riches and such joy that as to this all creatures must eternally be silent ; for the incomprehensible wonder of this love, eternally transcends the understanding of all creatures. But where this wonder is understood and tasted without amazement,   there the spirit dwells above itself, and is one with the Spirit of God ; and tastes and sees without measure, even as God, the riches which are the spirit itself in the unity of the living ground, where it possesses itself according to the way of its uncreated essence.

Now this rapturous meeting is incessantly and actively renewed in us, according to the way of God ; for the Father gives Himself in the Son, and the Son gives Himself in the Father, in an eternal content and a loving embrace ; and this renews itself every moment within the bonds of love. For like as the Father incessantly beholds all things in the birth of His Son, so all things are loved anew by the Father and the Son in the outpouring of the Holy Ghost. And this is the active meeting of the Father and of the Son, in which we are lovingly embraced by the Holy Ghost in eternal love.

Now this active meeting and this loving embrace are in their ground fruitive and wayless ; for the abysmal Waylessness of God is so dark and so unconditioned that it swallows up in itself every Divine way and activity, and all the attributes of the Persons, within the rich compass of the essential Unity ; and it brings about a Divine fruition in the abyss of the Ineffable. And here there is a death in fruition, and a melting and dying into the Essential Nudity, where all the Divine names, and all conditions, and all the living images which are reflected in the mirror of Divine Truth, lapse in the Onefold and Ineffable, in waylessness and without reason. For in this unfathomable abyss of the Simplicity, all things are wrapped in fruitive bliss ; and the abyss itself may not be comprehended, unless by the Essential Unity. To this the Persons, and all that lives in God, must give place ; for here there is nought else but an eternal rest in the fruitive embrace of an outpouring Love. And this is that wayless being which all interior spirits have chosen above all other things. This is the dark silence in which all lovers lose themselves. But if we would prepare ourselves for it by means of the virtues, we should strip ourselves of all but our very bodies, and should flee forth into the wild Sea, whence no created thing can draw us back again.

May we possess in fruition the essential Unity, and clearly behold unity in the Trinity; this may Divine Love, which turns no beggar away, bestow upon us. AMEN.

HERE ENDS THE BOOK OF THE ADORNMENT OF
THE SPIRITUAL MARRIAGE

THE SPARKLING STONE

THE SPARKLING STONE

PROLOGUE

THE man who would live in the most perfect state of Holy Church must be a good and zealous man ; an inward and ghostly man ; an uplifted and God-seeing man ; and an outflowing man to all in common. Whenever these four things are together in a man, then his state is perfect ; and through the increase of grace he shall continually grow and progress in all virtues, and in the knowledge of truth, before God and before all men.

CHAPTER I

THROUGH THREE THINGS A MAN BECOMES GOOD

HEAR now three things which constitute a good man. The first, which a good man must have, is a clean conscience without reproach of mortal sin. And therefore whosoever wishes to become a good man must examine and prove himself with due discernment, from that time onward when he could first have committed sin. And from all these sins he must purge himself, according to the precept and the custom of Holy Church.

The second thing which pertains to a good man is that he must in all things be obedient to God, and to Holy Church, and to his own proper convictions.

And to each of these three he must be equally obedient :
so shall he live without care and doubt, and shall ever
abide without inward reproach in all his deeds.

The third thing which behoves every good man is
that in all his deeds he should have in mind, above all
else, the glory of God. And if it happens that by
reason of his business or the multiplicity of his works,
he has not always God before his eyes, yet at least
there should be established in him the intention and
desire to live according to the dearest will of God.

Behold, these three things, when they are possessed
in this way, make a man good. And whosoever lacks
any one of these three is neither good nor in the
grace of God ; but whenever a man resolves in his
heart to fulfil these three points, how wicked soever he
may have been before, in that very instant he becomes
good, and is susceptible of God, and filled with the
grace of God.

CHAPTER II

THROUGH THREE THINGS A MAN BECOMES INWARD

IF, further, this good man would become an inward and
ghostly man, he needs must have three further things.
The first is a heart unencumbered with images ; the
second is spiritual freedom in his desires, the third is
the feeling of inward union with God.

Now let every one who thinks himself to be ghostly
observe himself. He who would have a heart void
of images may not possess anything with affection,
nor may he cling to any one, or have intercourse with
him with attachment of the will ; for all intercourse
and all affection which do not aim purely at the

honour of God bring images into a man's heart, since they are born, not of God, but of the flesh. And so if a man would become spiritual, he must forsake all fleshly lusts and loves and must cleave with longing and love to God alone, and thus possess Him. And through this, all imaginations and all inordinate love towards creatures are cast out. And this loving possession of God makes a man inwardly free from ungodly images ; for God is a Spirit, of Whom no one can make to himself a true image. Certainly in this exercise a man should lay hold of good images to help him ; such as the Passion of our Lord and all those things that may stir him to greater devotion. But in the possession of God, the man must sink down to that imageless Nudity which is God ; and this is the first condition, and the foundation, of a ghostly life.

The second condition is inward freedom. Through this, the man should be able to raise himself towards God in all inward exercises, free from images and encumbrances ; that is, in thanksgiving and praise, in worship, in devout prayer and fervent love, and in all those things that may be done by longing and love with the help of the grace of God and through inward zeal in all ghostly exercises.

Through this inward exercise, he reaches the third state ; which is that he feels a ghostly union with God. Whosoever then has, in his inward exercise, an imageless and free ascent unto his God, and means nought else but the glory of God, must taste of the goodness of God ; and he must feel from within a true union with God. And in this union, the inward and spiritual life is made perfect ; for in this union, the desirous power is perpetually enticed anew and stirred to new inward activity. And by each act, the spirit rises upwards to a new union. And so activity and union perpetually renew themselves; and this perpetual renewal in activity and in union is a ghostly life. And so you are now able to see how a man becomes good through the moral virtues and an upright intention; and how he may become ghostly through the inward virtues and union with God. But without these said points, he can neither be good nor ghostly.

CHAPTER III

THROUGH THREE THINGS A MAN BECOMES GOD-SEEING

FURTHER, you must know that if this ghostly man would now become a God-seeing man, he needs must have three other things. The first is the feeling that the foundation of his being is abysmal, and he should possess it in this manner; the second is that his inward exercise should be wayless; the third is that his indwelling should be a divine fruition.

Now understand, you who would live in the spirit, for I am speaking to no one else. The union with God which a spiritual man feels, when the union is revealed to the spirit as being abysmal—that is, measureless depth, measureless height, measureless length and measureless breadth—in this manifestation the spirit perceives that through love it has plunged itself into the depth and has ascended into the height and escaped into the length; and it feels itself to be wandering in the breadth, and to dwell in a knowledge which is ignorance. And through this intimate feeling of union, it feels itself to be melting into the Unity; and, through dying to all things, into the life of God. And there it feels itself to be one life with God. And this is the foundation, and the first point, of the God-seeing life.

And from this there arises the second point, which is an exercise above reason and without condition : for the Divine Unity, of which every God-seeing spirit has entered into possession in love, eternally draws and invites the Divine Persons and all loving spirits into its self. And this inward drawing is felt by each lover, more or less, according to the measure of his love and the manner of his exercise. And whosoever yields himself to this indrawing, and keeps himself therein, cannot fall into mortal sin. But the God-seeing man who has forsaken self and all things, and does not feel himself drawn away because he no longer possesses anything as his own, but stands empty of all, he can always enter, naked and unencumbered with images, into the inmost part of his spirit. There he finds revealed an Eternal Light; and in this light, he feels the eternal demand of the Divine Unity ; and he feels himself to be an eternal fire of love, which craves above all else to be one with God. The more he yields to this indrawing or demand, the more he feels it. And the more he feels it, the more he craves to be one with God ; for it urges him to pay the debt which is demanded of him by God. This eternal demand of the Divine Unity kindles within the spirit an eternal fire of love ; and though the spirit incessantly pays the debt, an eternal burning continues within it. For, in the transformation within the Unity, all spirits fail in their own activity, and feel nothing else but a burning up of themselves in the simple Unity of God. This simple Unity of God none can feel or possess save he who maintains himself in the immeasurable radiance, and in the love which is above reason and wayless. In this transcendent state the spirit feels in itself the eternal fire of love ; and in this fire of love it finds neither beginning nor end, and it feels itself one with this fire of love. The spirit for ever continues to burn in itself, for its love is eternal ; and it feels itself ever more and more to be burnt up in love, for it is drawn and transformed into the Unity of God, where the spirit burns in love. If it observes itself, it finds a distinction and an otherness between itself and God ; but where it is burnt up it is undifferentiated and without distinction, and therefore it feels nothing but unity ; for the flame of the Love of God consumes and devours all that it can enfold in its Self.

And thus you may see that the indrawing Unity of God is nought else than the fathomless Love, which lovingly draws inward, in eternal fruition, the Father and the Son and all that lives in Them. And in this Love we shall burn and be burnt up without end, throughout eternity ; for herein lies the blessedness of all spirits. And therefore we must all found our lives upon a fathomless abyss ; that we may eternally plunge into Love, and sink down in the fathomless Depth. And with that same Love, we shall ascend, and transcend ourselves, in the incomprehensible Height. And in that Love which is wayless, we shall wander and stray, and it shall lead us and lose us in the immeasurable Breadth of the Love of God. And herein we shall flee forth and flee out of ourselves, into the unknown raptures of the Goodness and Riches of God. And therein we shall melt and be melted away, and shall eternally wander and sojourn within the Glory of God. Behold! by each of these images, I show forth to God-seeing men their being and their exercise, but none else can understand them. For the contemplative life cannot be taught. But where the Eternal Truth reveals Itself within the spirit all that is needful is taught and learnt.

CHAPTER IV

OF THE SPARKLING STONE, AND OF THE NEW NAME WRITTEN IN THE BOOK OF THE SECRETS OF GOD

AND therefore the Spirit of our Lord speaks thus in the Book of the Secrets of God, which St John wrote down : TO HIM THAT OVERCOMETH, He says, that is, to him who overcometh and conquereth himself and all else, WILL I GIVE TO EAT OF THE HIDDEN MANNA, that is, an inward and hidden savour and celestial joy ; AND WILL GIVE HIM A SPARKLING STONE, AND IN THE STONE A NEW NAME WRITTEN WHICH NO MAN KNOWETH SAVING HE THAT RECEIVETH IT. This stone is called a pebble, for it is so small that it does not hurt when one treads on it. This stone is shining white and red like a flame of fire ; and it is small and round, and smooth all over, and very light. By this sparkling stone we mean our Lord Christ Jesus, for He is, according to His Godhead, a shining forth of the Eternal Light, and an irradiation of the glory of God, and a flawless mirror in which all things live. Now to him who overcomes and transcends all things, this sparkling stone is given ; and with it he receives light and truth and life. This stone is also like to a fiery flame, for the fiery love of the Eternal Word has filled the whole world with love and wills that all loving spirits be burned up to nothingness in love. This stone is also so small that a man hardly feels it, even though he treads it underfoot. And that is why it is called CALCULUS, that is, " treadling." And this is made clear to us by St Paul, where he says that the Son of God EMPTIED HIMSELF, AND HUMBLED HIMSELF, AND TOOK UPON HIM THE FORM OF A SERVANT, AND BECAME OBEDIENT UNTO DEATH, EVEN THE DEATH OF THE CROSS. And He Himself spoke through the mouth of the Prophet, saying : I AM A WORM, AND NO MAN : A REPROACH OF MEN AND DESPISED OF THE PEOPLE. And He made Himself so small in time that the Jews trod Him under their feet. But they felt Him not ; for, had they recognized the Son of God, they had not dared to crucify Him. He is still little and despised in all men's hearts that do not love Him well. This noble stone of which I speak is wholly round and smooth and even all over. That the stone is round teaches us that the Divine Truth has neither beginning nor end ; that it is smooth and even all over teaches us that the Divine Truth shall weigh all things evenly, and shall give to each according to his merits ; and that which he gives shall be with each throughout eternity. The last property of this stone of which I will speak is, that it is particularly light ; for the Eternal Word of the Father has no weight, nevertheless It bears heaven and earth by Its strength. And It is equally near to all things ; yet none can attain It, for It is set on high and goes before all creatures, and reveals Itself where

It wills and when It wills ; and, in Its lightness, our heavy human nature has climbed above all the heavens, and sits crowned at the right hand of the Father.

Behold, this is the sparkling stone which is given to the God-seeing man, and in this stone A NEW NAME IS WRITTEN, WHICH NO MAN KNOWETH SAVING HE THAT RECEIVETH IT. You should know that all spirits in their return towards God receive names ; each one in particular, according to the nobleness of its service and the loftiness of its love. For only the first name of innocence, which we receive at baptism, is adorned with the merits of our Lord Jesus Christ. And when we have lost this name of innocence through sin, if we are willing still to follow God—especially in three works which He wishes to work in us—we are baptized once more in the Holy Ghost. And thereby we receive a new name which shall remain with us throughout eternity.

CHAPTER V

OF THE WORKS WHICH GOD WORKS IN ALL IN COMMON AND OF FIVE KINDS OF SINNERS

HEAR now what those three works are, which our Lord works in all men if they will submit themselves thereto. The first work which God works in all men in common consists in His calling and inviting them all, without exception, to union with Himself. And as long as a sinner does not follow this call, he must lack all the other gifts which would follow thereafter.

Now I have observed that all sinners may be divided into five kinds. To the first kind belong all those who are careless of good works, who through bodily ease and the lust of the senses prefer to live in worldly employments and in multiplicity of heart. All such are unfit to receive the grace of God, and even if they had received it, they would not be able to keep it.

To the second kind belong those who have willingly and wittingly fallen into mortal sin, yet also do good works, and dwell in the fear and awe of the Lord, and love the just, and desire their prayers, and put their trust therein. So long, however, as turning from God and love of sin vanquish and repulse love of God and turning to God, so long these remain unworthy of the grace of God.

The third kind of sinners consists in all unbelievers, and those who err in faith. What good works soever they do, or what lives soever they lead, without the true faith they cannot please God ; for true faith is the foundation of all holiness and all virtues.

To the fourth kind belong those who abide in mortal sin without fear and without shame, who care not for God and His gifts, and neglect all virtues. They hold all ghostly life to be hypocrisy and deceit ; and they hardly listen to all that one may say to them of God or of the virtues, for they have established themselves as though there were no God, nor heaven, nor hell, and therefore they desire to know of nothing but that which they now perceive and have before them. Behold, all such are rejected and despised by God, for they sin against the Holy Ghost. Yet they may be converted ; but this happens with difficulty and seldom.

The fifth kind of sinners are those hypocrites who do outward good works, not for the glory of God and their own salvation, but to acquire a name for holiness, or for the sake of some fleeting thing. Though they may appear holy and good from without, within they are false and turned away from God, and they lack the grace of God and every virtue.

See, I have shown to you five kinds of sinners, who have all been inwardly called to union with God. But so long as a sinner remains in the service of sin, so long he remains deaf and blind and unable to taste, or to feel, all the good that God wishes to work in him. But whenever a sinner enters into himself, and considers himself, if he be displeased by his sinful life, then he draws near to God. But if he would be obedient to the call and the words of God, he must of his own free will resolve to leave sin and to do penance. And so he becomes one aim and one will with God, and receives the grace of God.

And therefore we should all conceive of God in this way : First of all that, of His free goodness, He calls and invites all men, without distinction, to union with Himself ; both the good and the wicked, without exception. Secondly, we should thus comprehend the goodness of God ; how He through grace flows forth towards all men who are obedient to the call of God. Thirdly, we should find and understand clearly in ourselves that we can become one life and one spirit with God, when we renounce ourselves in every way, and follow the grace of God to the height whereto it would guide us. For the grace of God works according to order in every man, after the measure and the way in which he is able to receive it. And thereby, through the universal working of the grace of God, every sinner, if he desires it, receives the discernment and strength which are needful, that he may leave sin and turn towards virtue. And, through that hidden co-operation of the grace of God, every good man can overcome all sins, and can resist all temptations, and can fulfil all virtues, and can persevere in the highest perfection, if he be in all things submissive to the grace of God. For all that we are, and all that we have received, from without and from within, these are all the free gifts of God ; for which we must thank and praise Him, and with which we must serve Him, if we are to please Him. But there are many gifts of God which are for the good an aid to, and a source of, virtue ; but for the wicked an aid to, and an occasion of, sin : such are health, beauty, wisdom, riches, and worldly dignity. These are the lowest and least precious gifts of God, which God gives for the benefit of all, to His friends and to His enemies, to the good and to the wicked. And with these the good serve God and His friends ; but the wicked, their own flesh, and the devil, and the world.

CHAPTER VI

OF THE DIFFERENCE BETWEEN THE HIRELINGS AND THE FAITHFUL SERVANTS OF GOD

Now you may mark this : that some men receive the gifts of God as hirelings, but others as faithful servants of God ; and these differ one from another in all inward works, that is, in love and intention, in feeling, and in every exercise of the inward life.

Now understand this well : all those who love themselves so inordinately that they will not serve God, save for their own profit and because of their own reward, these separate themselves from God, and dwell in bondage and in their own selfhood ; for they seek, and aim at, their own, in all that they do. And therefore, with all their prayers and with all their

good works, they seek after temporal things, or may
be strive after eternal things for their own benefit
and for their own profit. These men are bent upon
themselves in an inordinate way; and that is why
they ever abide alone with themselves, for they lack
the true love which would unite them with God
and with all His beloved. And although these men
seem to keep within the law and the commandments
of God and of Holy Church, they do not keep within
the law of love; for all that they do, they do, not
out of love, but from sheer necessity, lest they shall be
damned. And, because they are inwardly unfaithful,
they dare not trust in God; but their whole inward
life is doubt and fear, travail and misery. For they see
on the right hand eternal life, and this they are
afraid of losing; and they see on the left hand the
eternal pains of hell, and these they are afraid of
gaining. But all their prayers, all their labour and
all the good works, whatsoever they do, to cast out
this fear, help them not; for the more inordinately
they love themselves, the more they fear hell. And
from this you may learn that their fear of hell springs
from self-love, which seeks its own.

Now the Prophet, and also the Preacher, say : THE
FEAR OF THE LORD IS THE BEGINNING OF WISDOM;
but by this is meant that fear which is exercised
upon the right side, where one considers the loss of
eternal blessedness; for this fear arises from the
natural tendency which every man has in himself to
be blessed, that is, to see God. And therefore, even
though a man may be faithless to God, yet whenever
he truly observes himself from within, he feels himself
to be leaning out from himself towards that blessedness which is God. And this blessedness he fears to

lose ; for he loves himself better than God, and he loves blessedness wholly for his own sake. And therefore he dare not trust in God. And yet this is that FEAR OF THE LORD WHICH IS THE BEGINNING OF WISDOM, and is a law to the unfaithful servants of God : for it compels a man to leave sin, and to strive after virtue, and to do good deeds, and these things prepare a man from without to receive the grace of God and become a faithful servant.

But from that very hour in which, with God's help, he can overcome his selfhood—that is to say, when he is so detached from himself that he is able to leave in the keeping of God everything of which he has need—behold, through doing this he is so well pleasing to God that God bestows upon him His grace. And, through grace, he feels true love : and love casts out doubt and fear, and fills the man with hope and trust, and thus he becomes a faithful servant, and means and loves God in all that he does. Behold, this is the difference between the faithful servant and the hireling.

CHAPTER VII

OF THE DIFFERENCE BETWEEN THE FAITHFUL SERVANTS AND THE SECRET FRIENDS OF GOD

WE must now observe the great difference which there is between the faithful servants and the inward friends of God. For through grace and the help of God, the faithful servants have chosen to keep the commandments of God, that is, to be obedient to God and Holy Church in all virtues and goodly behaviour : and this is called the outward or active life. But the inward friends of God choose to follow, besides the commandments, the quickening counsels of God ; and this is a loving and inward cleaving to God for the sake of His eternal glory, with a willing abandonment of all that one may possess outside God with lust and love. All such friends God calls and invites inwards, and He teaches them the distinctions of inward exercises and many a hidden way of ghostly life. But He sends His servants outwards, that they may be faithful to Him and to His House in every service and in every kind of outward good works.

Behold, thus God gives His grace and His help to each man according to his fitness ; that is, according to the way in which he is in tune with God, whether in outward good works or in the inward practice of love. But none can do and feel the inward exercises unless he be wholly turned inward to God. For as long as a man is divided of heart, so long he looks outwards, and is unstable of mind, and is easily swayed by joy and grief in temporal things, for these are still alive within him. And though he may live according to the commandments of God, inwardly he abides in darkness, and knows not what inward exercises may be, nor how these should be practised. But, since he knows and feels that he has God in mind, and in all his works desires to fulfil His dearest will, with this he may be content ; for then he knows himself to be free from hypocrisy in his intention, and faithful in his service. And by these two things he contents himself ; and it seems to him that outward good works done with a pure intention are more holy and more profitable than any inward exercise whatever, for by the help of God, he has chosen an outward active way of virtue. And therefore he had rather exercise himself in the diversity of outward works than serve with inward love that same One for Whom he works. And that is the cause why his mind is more filled with the works which he does, than with God, for Whom he does them. And through · this tendency to images in his works, he remains an outward man, and is not able to follow the counsels of God ; for his exercise is more outward than inward, more of the senses than of the spirit. Though he is indeed a faithful servant of God in outward works, yet that which the secret friends of God experience remains hidden from, and unknown to him. And this is why certain gross and outward men always condemn and blame the inward and contemplative men, because they have in mind that these are idle. And this was also the reason why Martha complained to our Lord of her sister Mary, because she did not help her in serving ; for she believed that she was doing much service and much usefulness, and that her sister was sitting idle and doing nothing. But our Lord gave His judgment and decided between them : He did not blame Martha for her diligence, for her service was good and useful ; but He blamed her for her care, and because she was troubled and cast down by a multitude of outward things. And He praised Mary for her inward exercise, and said that One Thing was needful, and that she had chosen the better part, which should not be taken away from her.

That One Thing which is needful for all men is Divine love. The better part is an inward life, with loving adherence to God. This Mary Magdalen had chosen, and this is chosen by the secret friends of God. But Martha chose an outward, unenclosed, and active life ; and that is the other part, in which one may serve God, but which is neither so perfect nor so good. And this part is chosen out of love by the faithful servants of God.

But there are found some foolish men who would be so inward that they would neither act nor serve, even in those things of which their neighbour has need. Behold, these are neither secret friends nor faithful servants of God ; but they are altogether false and deceived. For no man can follow the counsels of God who will not keep His commandments. And therefore all secret friends of God are also at the same time faithful servants, wherever this is needful ; but all the faithful servants are not secret friends, for the exercise which belongs thereto is unknown to them.

This is the difference between the faithful servants and the secret friends of God.

CHAPTER VIII

OF THE DIFFERENCE BETWEEN THE SECRET FRIENDS AND THE HIDDEN SONS OF GOD

BUT further we find a more subtle and inward difference, between the secret friends and the hidden sons of God ; and yet both these alike by their inward exercise maintain themselves in the Presence of God. But the friends possess their inwardness as an attribute, for they choose the loving adherence to God as best and highest of all that they ever can and will reach : and that is why they cannot with themselves and their own activity penetrate to the imageless Nudity.

For they have, as images and intermediaries between God and themselves, their own being and their own activity. And though in their loving adherence they feel united with God, yet, in this union, they always feel a difference and an otherness between God and themselves. For the simple passing into the Bare and Wayless, they do not know and love : and therefore their highest inward life ever remains in Reason and in Ways. And though they have clear understanding and discernment of all virtues that may be conceived, the simple staring with open heart into the Divine Brightness remains unknown of them. And though they feel themselves uplifted to God in a mighty fire of love, yet they keep something of their own selfhood, and are not consumed and burnt to nothingness in the unity of love. And though they may desire to live for ever more in the service of God and to please Him eternally, they will not die in God to all the selfhood of their spirit, and receive from Him a God-formed life.   And even though they esteem little and count as nothing all consolation and all rest which may come from without, yet they greatly value the gifts of God, and also their own inward works, and the solace and sweetness which they feel within ; and thus they rest upon the way, and do not so wholly die to themselves, as to be able to attain the highest beatitude in bare and wayless love. And even if they could practise and apprehend with clear discernment the perfection of loving adherence to God, and all the inward and upward going ways by which one may pass into the Presence of God; yet the wayless passing, and the glorious wandering, in the Superessential Love, wherein neither end, nor beginning, nor way, nor manner, can ever be found, would remain hidden from, and unknown of them.

And so there is a great difference between the secret friends and the hidden sons of God. For the friends feel nought else but a loving and living ascent to God in some wise ; but, above this, the sons experience a simple and death-like passing which is in no wise.

The inward life of the friends of our Lord is an upward-striving exercise of love, wherein they desire to remain for ever with their own selfhood ; but how one possesses God through bare love above every exercise, in freedom from one's self, this they do not feel. Hence they are always striving upwards towards God in true faith, and await God and eternal blessedness with sincere hope, and are fastened and anchored to God through perfect charity. And therefore good things have befallen them, for they please God, and God is complaisant unto them : yet for all this, they are not assured of eternal life, for they have not entirely died to themselves and to all selfhood. But all those who abide and endure in their exercise and in that turning to God which they have chosen above all else, these God has chosen in eternity, and their names together with their works are written from eternity in the living book of the Providence of God. But those who choose other things, and turn their inward faces away from God toward sin, and endure therein (even though their names were written and known of God because of the temporal righteousness which they had practised before), their names shall be blotted out and erased from the Book of Life because they did not persevere unto death, and they shall never more be able to taste of God, nor of any fruit which springs from virtue. And therefore we must

needs observe ourselves with diligence, and adorn
our turning towards God, from within with inward
love, and from without with good works : thus we
can await in hope and joy the judgment of God and
the coming of our Lord Jesus Christ. But could
we renounce ourselves, and all selfhood in our works,
we should, with our bare and imageless spirit, transcend
all things : and, without intermediary, should be led
of the Spirit of God into the Nudity. And then we
should feel the certainty that we are indeed the sons
of God : for AS MANY AS ARE LED BY THE SPIRIT OF
GOD, THEY ARE THE SONS OF GOD, says the Apostle
St Paul.

Nevertheless, you should know that all good and
faithful men are the sons of God ; for they are all
born of the Spirit of God, and the Spirit of God
lives in them. And He moves and stirs them—each
according to his own capacity—to virtues and good
works, wherein they are well pleasing to God.   But
because of the inequality of their adherence and their
exercises, I call some the faithful servants of God,
and others I call His secret friends, and others again
His hidden sons : nevertheless, they are all servants,
friends, and sons, for they all serve and love and
mean one God, and they live and work only by the
free Spirit of God. And God permits and allows
that His friends do and leave undone all those things
which are not contrary to His commandments ; and
for those who are bound by the counsels of God,
then this bond also is a commandment. And so no
one is disobedient or contrary to God save he who
does not keep His commandments ; but all those
things which God commands and forbids in Scripture,
or by Holy Church, or in our conscience, all these

things we must do and leave undone, or else be disobedient to God, and lose His grace. But if we fall into venial sins, this is suffered both by God and by our reason, for we cannot wholly guard against them. And therefore such failings do not make us disobedient, for they do not drive out the grace of God nor our inward peace : nevertheless, we should always lament such lapses, how small soever they may be, and guard against them with all our might.

And by these words I have explained to you what I said at the beginning : namely, that every man must needs be obedient in all things to God and to Holy Church and to his own conscience ; for I do not wish that any should be unjustly offended by my words. And herewith I leave it even as I have said it.

CHAPTER IX

HOW WE MAY BECOME HIDDEN SONS OF GOD, AND ATTAIN TO THE GOD-SEEING LIFE

BUT I still longed to know how we may become hidden sons of God, and may attain to the God-seeing life. And as to this I have apprehended the following. As it has been said before, we must always live and be watchful in all virtues, and beyond all virtues must forsake this life and die in God ; for we must die to sin and be born of God into a life of virtue, and we must renounce ourselves and die in God into an eternal life. And as to this ensues the following instruction :

If we are born of the Spirit of God, we are the sons of grace ; and so our whole life is adorned with virtues.

Thereby we overcome all that is contrary to God; for St John says, WHATSOEVER IS BORN OF GOD OVERCOMETH THE WORLD. In this birth all good men are sons of God. And the Spirit of God kindles and stirs each one of them in particular to those virtues and to those good works for which he is in readiness, and of which he is capable. And so they please God all in common, and each in particular, according to the measure of his love and the nobleness of his exercise; nevertheless, they do not feel established nor possessed of God, nor assured of eternal life, for they may still turn away and fall into sin. And that is why I call them rather servants and friends, than sons. But when we transcend ourselves, and become, in our ascent towards God, so simple that the naked love in the height can lay hold of us, where love enfolds love, above every exercise of virtue—that is, in our Origin, of Which we are spiritually born—then we cease, and we and all our selfhood die in God. And in this death we become hidden sons of God, and find a new life within us: and that is eternal life. And of these sons, St Paul says: YOU ARE DEAD, AND YOUR LIFE IS HID WITH CHRIST IN GOD.

Now understand, the explanation of this is as follows. In our approach to God, we must carry with us ourselves and all our works, as a perpetual sacrifice to God; and in the Presence of God, we must forsake ourselves and all our works, and, dying in love, go forth from all creatureliness into the superessential richness of God: there we shall possess God in an eternal death to ourselves. And that is why the Spirit of God says in the book of the Divine Secrets: BLESSED ARE THE DEAD WHICH DIE IN THE LORD. Justly He calls them the blessed dead, for they remain

eternally dead and lost to themselves in the fruitive
Unity of God. And they die in love ever anew, through
the indrawing transformation of that same Unity.
Further, the Spirit of God says: THEY MAY REST
FROM THEIR LABOURS, AND THEIR WORKS DO FOLLOW
THEM. In the ordinary state of grace, when we are
born of God into a ghostly and virtuous life, we carry
our works before us, as an offering to God; but in
the wayless state, where we die back into God in an
eternal and blessed life, there our good works follow
us, for they are one life with us. When we go towards
God by means of the virtues, God dwells in us; but
when we go out from ourselves and from all else, then
we dwell in God. So soon as we have faith, hope
and charity, we have received God, and He dwells
in us with His grace, and He sends us out as His
faithful servants, to keep His commandments. And
He calls us in again as His secret friends, so soon as
we are willing to follow His counsels; and He names
us openly as His sons so soon as we live in opposition
to the world. But if above all things we would
taste God, and feel eternal life in ourselves, we must
go forth into God with our feeling, above reason; and
there we must abide, onefold, empty of ourselves, and
free from images, lifted up by love into the simple
bareness of our intelligence. For when we go out
in love beyond and above all things, and die to all
observation in ignorance and in darkness, then we are
wrought and transformed through the Eternal Word,
Who is the Image of the Father. In this idleness of
our spirit, we receive the Incomprehensible Light, which
enwraps us and penetrates us, as the air is penetrated
by the light of the sun. And this Light is nothing else
than a fathomless staring and seeing. What we are,

that we behold; and what we behold, that we are: for our thought, our life, and our being are uplifted in simplicity, and made one with the Truth which is God. And therefore in this simple staring we are one life and one spirit with God: and this I call a contemplative life. As soon as we cleave to God through love, we practise the better part; but when we gaze thus into our superessence, we possess God utterly. With this contemplation, there is bound up an exercise which is wayless, that is to say, a noughting of life; for, where we go forth out of ourselves into darkness and the abysmal Waylessness, there shines perpetually the simple ray of the Splendour of God, in which we are grounded, and which draws us out of ourselves into the superessence, and into the immersion of love. And with this sinking into love there is always bound up a practice of love which is wayless; for love cannot be lazy, but would search through and through and taste through and through the fathomless richness which lives in the ground of her being, and this is a hunger which cannot be appeased. But a perpetual striving after the unattainable—this is swimming against the stream. One can neither leave it nor grasp it, neither do without it nor attain it, neither be silent on it nor speak of it, for it is above reason and understanding, and it transcends all creatures; and therefore we can never reach nor overtake it. But we should abide within ourselves: there we feel that the Spirit of God is driving us and enkindling us in this restlessness of love. And we should abide above ourselves. And then we feel that the Spirit of God is drawing us out of ourselves and burning us to nothingness in His Selfhood; that is, in the Superessential Love with which we are one, and which we possess more deeply and more widely than all else.

This possession is a simple and abysmal tasting of all good and of eternal life; and in this tasting we are swallowed up above reason and without reason, in the deep Quiet of the Godhead, which is never moved. That this is true we can only know by our own feeling, and in no other way. For how this is, or where, or what, neither reason nor practice can come to know: and therefore our ensuing exercise always remains wayless, that is, without manner. For that abysmal Good which we taste and possess, we can neither grasp nor understand; neither can we enter into it by ourselves or by means of our exercises. And so we are poor in ourselves, but rich in God; hungry and thirsty in ourselves, drunken and fulfilled in God; busy in ourselves, idle in God. And thus we shall remain throughout eternity. But without the exercise of love, we can never possess God; and whosoever thinks or feels otherwise is deceived. And thus we live wholly in God, where we possess our blessedness; and we live wholly in ourselves, where we exercise ourselves in love towards God. And though we live wholly in God and wholly in ourselves, yet it is but one life; but it is twofold and opposite according to our feeling, for poor and rich, hungry and satisfied, busy and idle, these things are wholly contrary to one another. Yet with this our highest honour is bound up, now and in eternity: for we cannot wholly become God and lose our created being, this is impossible. Did we, however, remain wholly in ourselves, sundered from God, we should be miserable and unblest. And therefore we should feel ourselves living wholly in God and wholly in ourselves; and between these

two feelings we should find nothing else but the grace
of God and the exercise of our love.   For out of our
highest feeling, the brightness of God shines into us,
which teaches us truth, and moves us towards every
virtue and in eternal love towards God.   If we follow
this brightness without pause, back into that Source
from whence it comes forth, there we feel nothing but
a quenching of our spirit and an irretrievable down-
sinking into simple and fathomless love.   Could we
continue to dwell there with our simple gaze, we
should always so feel it ;   for our immersion and
transformation in God continues without ceasing in
eternity, if we have gone forth from ourselves, and
God is ours in the immersion of love.   For if we
possess God in the immersion of love—that is, if we
are lost to ourselves—God is our own and we are His
own :   and we sink ourselves eternally and irretriev-
ably in our own possession, which is God.   This
immersion is essential, and is closely bound up with
the state of love :   and so it continues whether we
sleep or whether we wake, whether we know it or
whether we know it not.   And so it does not earn for
us any new degree of reward ;   but it maintains us in
the possession of God and of all that good which we
have received.   And this down-sinking is like a river,
which without pause or turning back ever pours into
the sea ;   since this is its proper resting-place.   So
likewise when we possess God alone, the down-
sinking of our being, with the love that belongs to it,
flows forth, without return, into a fathomless experience which we possess, and which is our proper
resting-place.   Were we always simple, and could
we always contemplate with the same recollection,
we should always have the same experience.   Now

this immersion is above all virtues, and above every exercise of love ; for it is nothing else than an eternal going out from ourselves, with a clear looking forward, into an otherness or difference towards which, outside ourselves, we tend as towards our blessedness. For we feel an eternal yearning toward something other than what we are ourselves. And this is the most inward and hidden distinction which we can feel between God and ourselves, and beyond it there is no difference any more. But our reason abides here with open eyes in the darkness, that is, in an abysmal ignorance ; and in this darkness, the abysmal splendour remains covered and hidden from us, for its overwhelming unfathomableness blinds our reason. But it enwraps us in simplicity, and transforms us through its selfhood : and thus we are brought forth by God, out of our selfhood, into the immersion of love, in which we possess blessedness, and are one with God.

When we are thus made one with God, there abides within us a quickening knowledge and an active love ; for without our own knowledge, we cannot possess God ; and without the practice of love, we cannot be united with God, nor remain one with Him. For if we could be blessed without our knowledge, then a stone, which has no knowledge, could also be blessed. Were I lord over all the world and knew it not, how would it profit me ? And therefore we shall ever know and feel that we taste and possess ; and this is testified by Christ Himself, where He speaks thus of us to His Father : THIS, He says, IS LIFE ETERNAL, THAT THEY SHOULD KNOW THEE, THE ONLY TRUE GOD, AND JESUS CHRIST, WHOM THOU HAST SENT. And by this you may understand that our eternal life consists in knowledge with discernment.

CHAPTER X

HOW WE, THOUGH ONE WITH GOD, MUST ETERNALLY REMAIN OTHER THAN GOD

THOUGH I have said before that we are one with God, and this is taught us by Holy Writ, yet now I will say that we must eternally remain other than God, and distinct from Him, and this too is taught us by Holy Writ. And we must understand and feel both within us, if all is to be right with us.

And therefore I say further : that from the Face of God, or from our highest feeling, a brightness shines upon the face of our inward being, which teaches us the truth of love and of all virtues : and especially are we taught in this brightness to feel God and ourselves in four ways. First, we feel God in His grace ; and when we apprehend this, we cannot remain idle. For like as the sun, by its splendour and its heat, enlightens and gladdens and makes fruitful the whole world, so God does to us through His grace : He enlightens and gladdens and makes fruitful all men who desire to obey Him. If, however, we would feel God within us, and have the fire of His love ever more burning within us, we must, of our own free will, help to kindle it in four ways : We must abide within ourselves, united with the fire through inwardness. And we must go forth from ourselves towards all good men with loyalty and brotherly love. And we must go beneath ourselves in penance, betaking ourselves to all good works, and resisting our inordinate lusts. And we must ascend above ourselves with the flame of this fire, through devotion, and thanksgiving, and praise, and fervent prayer, and must ever cleave to God with an upright intention and with sensible love. And thereby God continues to dwell in us with His grace ; for in these four ways is comprehended every exercise which we can do with the reason, and in some wise, but without this exercise no one can please God. And he who is most perfect in this exercise, is nearest to God. And therefore it is needful for all men ; and above it none can rise save the contemplative men. And thus, in this first way, we feel God within us through His grace, if we wish to belong to Him.

Secondly : when we possess the God-seeing life, we feel ourselves to be living *in* God ; and from out of that life in which we feel God in ourselves, there shines forth upon the face of our inward being a brightness which enlightens our reason, and is an intermediary between ourselves and God. And if we with our enlightened reason abide within ourselves in this brightness, we feel that our created life incessantly immerses itself in its eternal life. But when we follow the brightness above reason with a simple sight, and with a willing leaning out of ourselves, toward our highest life, there we experience the transformation of our whole selves in God ; and thereby we feel ourselves to be wholly enwrapped in God.

And, after this, there follows the third way of feeling ; namely, that we feel ourselves to be one *with* God ; for, through the transformation in God, we feel ourselves to be swallowed up in the fathomless abyss of our eternal blessedness, wherein we can nevermore find any distinction between ourselves and God. And this is our highest feeling, which we cannot experience in any other way than in the immersion in love. And therefore, so soon as we are uplifted and drawn into our highest feeling, all our powers stand

idle in an essential fruition ; but our powers do not
pass away into nothingness, for then we should lose
our created being. And as long as we stand idle,
with an inclined spirit, and with open eyes, but without reflection, so long we can contemplate and have
fruition. But, at the very moment in which we seek
to prove and to comprehend what it is that we feel,
we fall back into reason, and there we find a distinction and an otherness between ourselves and God,
and find God outside ourselves in incomprehensibility.

And hence the fourth way of distinction ; which
is, that we feel God *and* ourselves. Hereby we now
find ourselves standing in the Presence of God ; and
the truth which we receive from the Face of God
teaches us that God would be wholly ours and that He
wills us to be wholly His. And in that same moment
in which we feel that God would be wholly ours, there
arises within us a gaping and eager craving which
is so hungry and so deep and so empty that, even
though God gave all that He could give, if he gave
not Himself, we should not be appeased. For, whilst
we feel that He has given Himself and yielded Himself
to our untrammeled craving, that we may taste of
Him in every way that we can desire—and of this we
learn the truth in His sight—yet all that we taste,
against all that we lack, is but like to a single drop
of water against the whole sea : and this makes our
spirit burst forth in fury and in the heat and the rest-
lessnesss of love. For the more we taste, the greater
our craving and our hunger ; for the one is the cause of
the other. And thus it comes about that we struggle
in vain. For we feed upon His Immensity, which
we cannot devour, and we yearn after His Infinity,
which we cannot attain : and so we cannot enter

into God nor can God enter into us, for in the un-
tamed fury of love we are not able to renounce ourselves. And therefore the heat is so unmeasured
that the exercise of love between ourselves and God
flashes to and fro like the lightning in the sky; and
yet we cannot be consumed in its ardour. And in
this storm of love our activity is above reason and
wayless; for love longs for that which is impossible
to it, and reason teaches that love is in the right, but
reason can neither counsel love nor dissuade her. For
as long as we inwardly perceive that God would be
ours, the goodness of God touches our eager craving :
and therefrom springs the wildness of love, for the
touch which pours forth from God stirs up this wildness, and demands our activity, that is, that we
should love eternal love. But the inward-drawing
touch draws us out of ourselves, and calls us to be
melted and noughted in the Unity. And in this
inward-drawing touch, we feel that God wills us to be
His ; and therefore, we must renounce ourselves and
leave Him to work our blessedness. But where He
touches us by the outpouring touch, He leaves us to
ourselves, and makes us free, and sets us in His
Presence, and teaches us to pray in the spirit and to
ask in freedom, and shows us His incomprehensible
riches in such manifold ways as we are able to grasp.
For everything that we can conceive, wherein is
consolation and joy, this we find in Him without
measure. And therefore, when our feeling shows
us that He with all these riches would be ours and
dwell in us for ever more, then all the powers of the
soul open themselves, and especially the desirous
power ; for all the rivers of the grace of God pour
forth, and the more we taste of them, the more we

long to taste; and the more we long to taste, the
more deeply we press into contact with Him; and
the more deeply we press into contact with God, the
more the flood of His sweetness flows through us and
over us; and the more we are thus drenched and
flooded, the better we feel and know that the sweetness of God is incomprehensible and unfathomable.
And therefore the prophet says : O TASTE, AND SEE
THAT THE LORD IS SWEET.   But he does not say how
sweet He is, for God's sweetness is without measure ;
and therefore we can neither grasp it nor swallow it.
And this is also testified by the bride of God in the
Song of Songs, where she says : I SAT DOWN UNDER HIS
SHADOW, WITH GREAT DELIGHT, AND HIS FRUIT WAS
SWEET TO MY TASTE.

CHAPTER XI

OF THE GREAT DIFFERENCE BETWEEN THE BRIGHTNESS OF THE SAINTS AND THE HIGHEST BRIGHTNESS TO WHICH WE CAN ATTAIN IN THIS LIFE

THERE is a great difference between the brightness
of the saints and the highest brightness or enlightenment to which we may attain in this life.   For it is
only the shadow of God which enlightens our inward
wilderness, but on the high mountains of the Promised
Land there is no shadow : and yet it is one and the
same Sun, and one radiance, which enlightens both
our wilderness and the high mountains.   But the
state of the saints is transparent and shining, and
therefore they receive the brightness without intermediary : but our state is still mortal and gross, and

The Sparkling Stone 213

this sets up an obstacle which causes the shadow, which so darkens our understanding that we cannot know God and heavenly things so clearly as the saints can and do. For as long as we dwell in the shadow, we cannot see the sun in itself; but Now WE SEE THROUGH A GLASS DARKLY, says St Paul. Yet the shadow is so enlightened by the sunshine that we can perceive the distinctions between all the virtues, and all the truth which is profitable to our mortal state. But if we would become one with the brightness of the Sun, we must follow love, and go out of ourselves into the Wayless, and then the Sun will draw us with our blinded eyes into Its own brightness, in which we shall possess unity with God. So soon we feel and understand ourselves thus, we are in that contemplative life which is within reach of our mortal state.

The state of the Jews, according to the Old Testament, was cold and in the night, and they walked in darkness. And they DWELT IN THE LAND OF THE SHADOW OF DEATH, says the prophet Isaias. The shadow of death came forth from original sin; and therefore they had all to endure the lack of God. But though our state in the Christian faith is but still in the cool and morning hour; yet for us the day has dawned. And therefore we shall walk in the light, and shall sit down in the shadow, of God; and His grace shall be an intermediary between ourselves and God. And, through it, we shall overcome all things, and shall die to all things, and shall pass without hindrance into the unity of God. But the state of the saints is warm and bright; for they live and walk in the noon-tide, and see with open and enlightened eyes the brightness of the Sun, for the glory of God flows through them and overflows in them. And each one according to the degree of his enlightenment, tastes and knows the fruits of all the virtues which have there been gathered together by all spirits. But that they taste and know the Trinity in the Unity, and the Unity in the Trinity, and know themselves united therewith, this is the highest and all-surpassing food which makes them drunken, and causes them to rest in Its Selfhood. And This it was that the bride in the Book of Love desired, when she said unto Christ : TELL ME, O THOU WHOM MY SOUL LOVETH, WHERE THOU FEEDEST, WHERE THOU MAKEST THY FLOCK TO REST AT NOON, that is, in the light of glory, as St Bernard says ; for all the food which is given to us here, in the morning hour and in the shadow, is but a foretaste of the food that is to come in the noon-tide of the glory of God.

Yet the bride of our Lord gloried in having sat under the shadow of God, and that His fruit was sweet to her taste. Whenever we feel that God touches us from within, we taste of His fruit and His food : for His touch is His food. And His touch is both indrawing and outpouring, as I have said before. In His indrawing, we must be wholly His : thereby we learn to die and to behold. But in His outpouring, He wills to be wholly ours : and then He teaches us to live in the riches of the virtues. In His indrawing-touch all our powers forsake us, and then we sit under His shadow, and His fruit is sweet to our taste, for the Fruit of God is the Son of God, Whom the Father brings forth in our spirit. This Fruit is so infinitely sweet to our taste that we can neither swallow It nor assimilate It, but It rather absorbs us into Itself and assimilates us with Itself.   And whenever this

Fruit draws us inward and touches us, we abandon, forsake, and overcome all other things. And in this overcoming of all things, we taste of the hidden manna, which shall give us eternal life ; for we receive the sparkling stone, of which I have spoken heretofore, in which our new names were written before the beginning of the world.

This is the NEW NAME WHICH NO MAN KNOWETH BUT HE THAT RECEIVETH IT. And whosoever feels himself to be for ever united with God, he possesses his name according to the measure of his virtues, and of his introversion, and of his union. And, that every one may obtain his name and possess it in eternity, the Lamb of God, that is, the manhood of our Lord, has delivered Itself up to death ; and has opened for us the Book of Life, wherein are written all the names of the elect. And these names cannot be blotted out, for they are one with the Living Book, which is the Son of God. And that same death has broken for us the seals of the Book, so that all virtues may be fulfilled according to the eternal Providence of God. And so, in the measure in which each man can overcome himself, and can die to all things, he feels the touch of the Father drawing him inward ; and then he tastes the sweetness of the Inborn Fruit, Which is the Son ; and in this tasting the Holy Ghost teaches him that he is the heir of God. But in these three points no one is like to another in every respect. And therefore each one has been named separately, and his name is continually made new through new graces and new works of virtue. And therefore every knee shall bow before the Name of Jesus, for He has fought for our sake, and has conquered. And He has enlightened our darkness, and has fulfilled all the virtues

in the highest degree.   And so His name is lifted up
above all other names, for He is the King and the
Prince over all the elect.   And in His name we are
called and chosen, and adorned with grace and with
virtues, and look for the glory of God.

CHAPTER XII

OF THE TRANSFIGURATION OF CHRIST ON
MOUNT THABOR

AND so, that the Name of Christ may be exalted and
glorified in us, we should follow Him up the mountain of
our bare intelligence,[1] even as Peter, James, and John
followed Him on to mount Thabor.   Thabor means
in our tongue an increase of light.   So soon as we are
like Peter in knowledge of truth, and like James in
the overcoming of the world, and like John in fulness
of grace possessing the virtues in righteousness ;   then
Jesus brings us up on to the mountain of our bare
intelligence to a hidden solitude, and reveals Himself
to us in glory and in Divine brightness.   And, in His
name, His Father in heaven opens to us the living
book of His Eternal Wisdom.   And the Wisdom of
God enfolds our bare vision and the simplicity of our
spirit in a wayless, simple fruition of all good without
distinction ;   and here there are indeed seeing and
knowing, tasting and feeling, essence and life, having
and being : and all this is one in our transcendence in
God.   And before this transcendence we are all set,

---

[1] Ruysbroeck wrote *"bloter ghedacten"* ; probably meaning the
simple and undifferentiated consciousness, above the discursive
reason, which is attained in high contemplative states ; the "pure
intellect" of Plotinus.

each in his own particular way; and our heavenly
Father, of His wisdom and goodness, endows each
one in particular according to the nobility of his life
and his practice.   And therefore, if we ever remained
with Jesus on mount Thabor, that is, upon the
mountain of our bare thought, we should continually
experience a growth of new light and new truth;
for we should ever hear the voice of the Father, Who
touches us, pouring forth with grace, and drawing us
inward into the unity.   The voice of the Father is
heard by all who follow our Lord Jesus Christ, for He
says of them all : " These are My chosen sons, in
whom I am well pleased."   And, through this good
pleasure, each one receives grace, according to the
measure and the way in which God is well-pleasing
unto him.   And therefrom, between our pleasure
in God, and God's pleasure in us, there arises the
practice of true love.   And so each one tastes of
his name and his office and the fruit of his exercise.
And here all good men abide, hidden from those who
live in the world ; for these are dead before God and
have no name, and therefore they can neither feel
nor taste that which belongs to those who live indeed.

The outpouring touch of God quickens us with life
in the spirit, and fulfills us with grace, and enlightens
our reason, and teaches us to know truth and to discern
the virtues, and keeps us stable in the Presence of
God, with such a great strength that we are able to
endure all the tasting, all the feeling, and all the outpouring gifts of God without our spirits failing us.
But the indrawing-touch of God demands of us, that
we should be one with God, and go forth from ourselves, and die into blessedness, that is, into the
Eternal Love Which embraces the Father and the

Son in one fruition. And therefore when we have climbed with Jesus on to the mountain of our bare thought; and if, then, we follow Him with a single and simple gaze, with inward pleasure, and with fruitive inclination, we feel the fierce heat of the Holy Ghost, burning and melting us into the Unity of God. For when we are one with the Son, and lovingly return towards our Beginning, then we hear the voice of the Father, touching us and drawing us inward; for He says to all His chosen in His Eternal Word: THIS IS MY BELOVED SON, IN WHOM I AM WELL PLEASED. For you should know that the Father with the Son, and the Son with the Father, have conceived an eternal satisfaction in regard to this: that the Son should take upon Himself our manhood, and die, and bring back all the chosen to their Beginning.

And so soon as we are uplifted through the Son into our Origin, we hear the voice of the Father, which draws us inward, and enlightens us with eternal truth. And truth shows to us the wide-opened good-pleasure of God, in which all good-pleasure begins and ends. There all our powers fail us, and we fall from ourselves into our wide-opened contemplation, and become all One and one All, in the loving embrace of the Threefold Unity. Whenever we feel this union, we are one being and one life and one blessedness with God. And there all things are fulfilled and all things are made new; for when we are baptized into the wide embrace of the Love of God, the joy of each one of us becomes so great and so special that he can neither think of nor care for the joy of anyone else; for then each one is himself a Fruition of Love, and he cannot and dare not seek for anything beyond his own.

CHAPTER XIII

HOW WE OUGHT TO HAVE FRUITION OF GOD

IF a man would have fruition of God, three things are needful thereto ; these are, true peace, inward silence, and loving adherence.

Whosoever would find true peace between himself and God must love God in such a way that he can, with a free heart, renounce for the glory of God everything which he does or loves inordinately, or which he possesses, or can possess, contrary to the glory of God. This is the first thing which is needful to all men.

The second thing is an inward silence ; that is, that a man should be empty and free from images of all things which he ever saw or of which he ever heard.

The third thing is a loving adherence to God, and this adherence is itself fruition ; for whosoever cleaves to God out of pure love, and not for his own profit, he enjoys God in truth, and feels that he loves God and that God loves him.

There are still three other points, which are higher still, and which establish a man and make him able to enjoy and to feel God continually, if it be His good will to have it so.

The first of these points is to rest in Him Whom one enjoys ; that is, where love is overcome by the lover, and love is taken possession of by the lover, in bare Essential Love. There love has fallen in love with the lover, and each is all to the other, in possession and in rest.

From this there follows the second : and this is

called a falling asleep in God ; that is, when the spirit immerses itself, and knows not how, nor where, nor in what it is.

And therefrom follows the last point that can be put into words, that is, when the spirit beholds a Darkness into which it cannot enter with the reason. And there it feels itself dead and lost to itself, and one with God without difference and without distinction. And when it feels itself one with God, then God Himself is its peace and its enjoyment and its rest. And this is an unfathomable abyss wherein man must die to himself in blessedness, and must live again in virtues, whenever love and its stirring demand it. Lo ! if you feel these six points within you, then you feel all that I have, or could have, said before. And introversion is as easy to you, and contemplation and fruition are as ready to you, as your life according to nature. And from these riches there comes that common life of which I promised to speak to you at the beginning.

CHAPTER XIV

OF THAT COMMON LIFE WHICH COMES FROM THE CONTEMPLATION AND FRUITION OF GOD

THE man who is sent down by God from these heights into the world is full of truth and rich in all virtues. And he seeks not his own but the glory of Him Who has sent him. And hence he is just and truthful in all things, and he possesses a rich and a generous ground, which is set in the richness of God : and therefore he must always spend himself on those who have need of him; for the living fount of the Holy Ghost, which is his wealth, can never be spent. And he is a living and willing instrument of God, with which God works whatsoever He wills and howsoever He wills; and these works he reckons not as his own, but gives all the glory to God. And so he remains ready and willing to do in the virtues all that God commands, and strong and courageous in suffering and enduring all that God allows to befall him. And by this he possesses a universal life, for he is ready alike for contemplation and for action, and is perfect in both of them. And none can have this universal life save the God-seeing man; and none can contemplate and enjoy God save he who has within himself the six points, ordered as I have described heretofore. And therefore, all those are deceived who fancy themselves to be contemplative, and yet inordinately love, practice, or possess, some creaturely thing; or who fancy that they enjoy God before they are empty of images, or that they rest before they enjoy. All such are deceived; for we must make ourselves fit for God with an open heart, with a peaceful conscience, with naked contemplation, without hypocrisy, in sincerity and truth. And then we shall mount up from virtue unto virtue, and shall see God, and shall enjoy Him, and in Him shall become one with Him, in the way which I have shown to you. That this be done in all of us, so help us God. AMEN.

THE BOOK OF SUPREME TRUTH

THE BOOK OF SUPREME TRUTH

PROLOGUE

THE prophet Samuel mourned for King Saul, though he knew well that God had rejected him and his issue from being kings in Israel: this was because of his pride, and because he did not obey God and the prophet who spoke in His name. We may also read in the Gospel, that the disciples of our Lord pleaded with Him for the Gentile woman of Canaan, to send her away, that is, to do unto her that which she desired; for she cried after Him. So likewise I might say that we must mourn for all such deceived men as think themselves to be kings in Israel; for they believe themselves to be lifted up above other good men, into a lofty and God-seeing life. And yet they are proud and wittingly and willingly disobedient to God and the law and the Holy Church and every virtue. And like as Saul rent the mantle of the prophet Samuel, they endeavour to rend asunder the unity of the Christian faith, and all true doctrine and virtuous life. Whosoever persist herein, they are separated and shut out from the kingdom of eternal contemplation, even as Saul was shut out from the kingdom of Israel. But that humble little woman of Canaan, though she was Gentile and a stranger, had faith and hope in God, and acknowledged and confessed her littleness before Christ and

His apostles : and so she received grace and health
and all that she desired.   For God exalts the humble,
and fills them with grace and all virtues ; and He
resists the proud, and these remain empty of all good.

CHAPTER I

WHEREFORE THIS BOOK WAS WRITTEN

CERTAIN of my friends have desired and besought
me, that I should show and make plain in a few
words and according to my best cunning, shortly
and clearly, how I understand and feel the truth of
all the highest teachings that I have written before ;
so that none should take offence at my words, but
everyone should profit by them.   And this I willingly
consent to do.   I will, with God's help, teach the
humble who love virtue and truth ; and, with the
same words, I shall inwardly vex and darken the
false and the proud : for to these my words will be
displeasing and contrary, and this the proud cannot
endure, but it provokes them to anger.

CHAPTER II

A SHORT REPETITION OF ALL THE HIGHEST TEACHINGS
WRITTEN BY THE AUTHOR

BEHOLD, I have said this : that the contemplative
lover of God is united with God through means, and
also without means, and thirdly, without difference
or distinction ; and this I find in nature, and in grace,

and also in glory. Further I have said that never creature may be or become so holy that it loses its created being and becomes God; even the soul of our Lord Jesus Christ shall ever remain creature, and other than God. Yet, none the less, we must all be lifted up above ourselves into God, and become one spirit with God in love; and then we shall be blessed. And therefore mark my words and my meaning, and understand me aright as to what is the condition and the way to our eternal blessedness.

CHAPTER III

OF THE UNION THROUGH MEANS

AND next, I will say that all good men are united with God through means. These means are the grace of God, and the sacraments of Holy Church, and the Divine virtues, faith, hope and charity, and a virtuous life according to the commandments of God; and to these there belongs a death to sin and to the world and to every inordinate lust of nature. And through these, we remain united with Holy Church, that is, with all good men; and with these, we obey God, and are one will with Him, even as an orderly convent is united with its Superior: and without this union none can please God nor be saved. Whosoever keeps this union through these means unto the end of his life, he shall be one of those of whom Christ says unto His Father in heaven in the Gospel of St John: FATHER, I WILL THAT THEY ALSO WHOM THOU HAST GIVEN ME BE WITH ME WHERE I AM: THAT THEY MAY BEHOLD MY GLORY WHICH THOU HAST

GIVEN ME. And in another place He says that HIS
SERVANTS SHALL SIT DOWN TO MEAT—that is, in the
richness and the fulness of those virtues which they
have exercised—and He will go one to another and
WILL MINISTER UNTO THEM of His glory which He has
achieved. And He will generously impart and reveal
to His beloved, to each one specially and separately—
more or less according as he is worthy of it and can
lay hold of it—the loftiness of His glory and honour,
which He alone has earned by the merits of His life
and His death. Thus all saints shall be forever
with Christ, each in his own order and in the degree
of glory which he has earned through God's help by
his works. And Christ, according to His manhood,
shall be set above all saints, and above all angels;
as a prince of all glory and all honour; the which
pertain to His manhood alone above all creatures.
Behold, thus you may understand how we are united
with God through means, both here in grace and
hereafter in glory. But there is a great distinction
and a great difference in these means, and this is true
both as regards life and reward, as I have told you.
And this was well understood by St Paul, when he
said that he had A DESIRE TO DEPART AND TO BE WITH
CHRIST. But he did not say that he had a desire to
be Christ Himself or God; as is done by some un-
believing and perverse men, who say that they have
no God, but that they are so wholly dead to themselves, and united with God, that they have themselves
become God.

CHAPTER IV

OF THE MEN WHO PRACTISE A FALSE VACANCY

BEHOLD, such folk, by means of a onefold simplification and a natural tendency, are turned in upon the
bareness of their own being ; and therefore they
think eternal life is and shall be nought else but an
enduring state of beatitude, without distinction in
order in holiness or in reward. Yea, all such are so
deep in error that they say that the Persons shall
pass away into the Godhead, and that nought else shall
remain in eternity than the essential substance of
the Godhead ; and that all blessed spirits shall be so
simply absorbed with God in the Essential Blessedness
that nothing shall remain beside it, neither willing
nor working; nor the discerning knowledge of any
creature whatsoever. Behold, these men have gone
astray into the vacant and blind simplicity of their
own being, and they seek for blessedness in bare
nature ; for they are so simply and so idly united
with the bare essence of their souls, and with that
wherein God always is, that they have neither zeal,
nor cleaving to God, neither from without, nor from
within. For in the highest part into which they
have entered, they feel nothing but the simplicity of
their own proper being, depending upon the Being
of God. And the onefold simplicity which they there
possess, they take to be God, because they find a
natural rest therein. And so they think themselves
to be God in their simple ground ; for they lack
true faith, hope and charity. And, because of the
naked emptiness which they feel and possess, they say
that they are without knowledge and without love,

and are exempt from the virtues. And so they endeavour to live without heeding their conscience, what wickedness soever they commit. And they are careless of the sacraments, and of all virtues, and of all the practices of Holy Church, and believe that they have no need of them : for they fancy in their folly that they have passed beyond all these things, but imperfect men, they say, have need of them. And some men have become so accustomed to and deep-rooted in this simplification that they would know and heed as little of all the works which God has wrought, and all that Scripture teaches, as though not one line had ever been written ; for they believe themselves to have found and to possess that for the sake of which all Scriptures have been made, namely, the blind essential rest which they feel. But in fact they have lost God and all the ways which may lead to Him ; for they have no more inwardness, nor more devotion, nor holy practices, than a dead beast has. Yet they sometimes approach the sacraments, and at times they quote the Scriptures, that thus they may the better dissimulate and cover themselves ; and they like to take some dark saying of Scripture, which they can falsely turn to their own sense, so that they may please other simple men, and may draw them into the false vacancy which they themselves feel. Behold, these folk think themselves wise and subtle beyond any one else, and yet they are the most coarse and crude of all men living ; for that which even Pagans and Jews and bad Christians, learned and unlearned, find and understand through their natural reason, these wretched men neither can nor will attain. You may cross yourselves against the devil, but beware earnestly

of these perverted men, and take care lest you should
not recognise them in their words and works. For
they would teach, and be taught of none ; they would
reprove, and be reproved of none ; they would command, and obey none. They would oppress others,
but no one may oppress them ; they wish to say
whatever they like, but will endure no contradiction ;
they recognise only their own self-will and are subject
to no one ; and this they take to be ghostly freedom.
They practise the liberty of the flesh, for they give
to the body whatsoever it lusts after ; and this they
take to be natural freedom. They have unified
themselves in a blind and dark vacancy of their
own being ; and there, they think, they are one with
God, and they take this for the Eternal Blessedness.
And they have entered into this, and have taken
possession of it, through self-will and their natural
tendency ; and therefore they imagine themselves
to be set above the law and above the commandments of God and Holy Church. For, above that
essential rest which they possess, they feel neither
God nor any otherness ; for the Divine light
has not shone into their dimness. And this is
because they have neither sought after it through
active love nor through supernatural freedom. And
thus they have lost truth and every virtue, and have
fallen into a perverted unlikeness ; for they make it
a part of the highest holiness that a man should yield
to all that concerns his nature, and be without re-
straint, so that he may abide, with an inclined
spirit, in vacancy ; and that as regards the lusts of
the flesh whenever they move him, he should turn
outwards, that the flesh being satisfied, he may quickly
escape from the image and may return once more

unencumbered into the bare vacancy of his spirit. Lo! this is a fruit of hell, which grows from their unbelief; and therewith shall unbelief be nourished even in death. For, when the time has come and their nature is weighed down with bitter woe and the sorrow of death, then they are filled with images and unrest and inward fear; and they lose their vacant introversion in quietude, and fall into such despair that none can console them, and they die like mad dogs. And their vacancy shall bring them no reward, and those who worked wicked works, and died in them, shall go to the eternal flames, as our faith teaches.

I have shown to you the evil and the good side by side, so that you may so much the better understand the good and be able to guard against the evil. You shall abhor and fly from such folk, for, how holy soever they seem in their conduct, in works, in dress and demeanour, they are the mortal enemies of your soul. For they are the devil's ministers, and the most noxious of all who now live to simple and unlearned men of good-will. But I will leave this subject, and go back again to the matter with which I first began.

CHAPTER V

OF THE UNION WITHOUT MEANS

You may remember that I showed heretofore how all saints and all good men are united with God through means. Now I will further show to you how they are all united with God without means. But in this life there are but few who are meet for this, and sufficiently enlightened to feel and understand it. And there-

fore, whosoever wishes to find and to feel within himself those three unions of which I am going to speak,
he must live entirely and wholly in God, so that he
may satisfy and be amenable to the grace and the
stirring of God, in all virtues and inward exercises.
And he must be lifted up through love, and die in
God to himself and all his works; so that he yields
himself up with all his powers, and submits to the
transformation through the incomprehensible Truth
which is God Himself. And to that end it is needful
that living he should go forth in the virtues, and dying
should enter into God. And in these two things his
perfect life consists; and these two are joined together within him like matter and form, like body and
soul. And as he exercises himself in them so he
becomes clear in understanding, and rich and overflowing in feeling; for he has joined himself to
God with uplifted powers, with true intention, with
his heart's desire, with ceaseless craving, with the
living ardour of his spirit and of his nature. And
since he thus exercises himself and keeps himself in
the Presence of God, love overpowers him: in whatsoever manner he moves, he is ever growing in love
and in all virtues. But love always moves each man
according to the profit and the ability of each.

CHAPTER VI

OF HEAVENLY WEAL AND HELLISH WOE

THE most profitable stirrings which such a man can
feel, and for which he is best fitted, are heavenly
weal and hellish woe, and the ability to respond to

these two with fit and proper works. For heavenly
weal lifts a man up above all things into an untrammelled power of praising and loving God in every
way that his heart and his soul desire. After this
comes hellish woe, and casts him down into a misery,
and into a lack of all the comfort and consolation that
he experienced before. In this woe, weal sometimes
shows itself, and brings with it a hope which none can
gainsay. And then the man falls back again into a
despair in which he can find no consolation. When a
man feels God within himself with rich and full grace,
this I call heavenly health; for then he is wise and
clear of understanding, rich and outflowing with
heavenly teachings, ardent and generous in charity,
drunken and overflowing with joy, strong in
feeling, bold and ever ready in all the things which
he knows to be well pleasing to God; and such-like
things without number, which may only be known
by those who feel them. But when the scale of love
goes down, and God hides Himself with all His graces,
then the man falls back into dereliction and torment
and dark misery, as though he should never more
recover: and then he feels himself to be nought else
but a poor sinner, who knows little or nothing of God.
He scorns every consolation that creatures may give
him; and the taste and consolation of God he does
not receive. And then his reason says within him:
WHERE IS NOW THY GOD? What hath become of all
that thou didst receive from God? Then his TEARS
ARE HIS MEAT DAY AND NIGHT, as the Prophet says.
Now if that man is to recover from this misery, he
must observe and feel that he does not belong to himself, but to God; and therefore he must freely abandon
his own will to the will of God, and must leave God

to work in him in time and in eternity. So soon
as he can do this, with untroubled heart, and with a
free spirit, at that very moment he recovers his health,
and brings heaven into hell, and hell into heaven.
For howsoever the scales of love go up and down,
all things to him are even or alike. For whatsoever
love gives or takes away, he who abandons himself
and loves God finds peace in all. For his spirit remains free and unmoved, who lives in all pains without rebellion; and he is able to feel the unmediated
union with God. For he has achieved the union
through means by the richness of his virtues. And
after this, because he is one aim and one will with
God, he feels God within himself together with the
fulness of His grace, as the quickening health of his
being and all his works.

CHAPTER VII

SHOWING WHEREFORE ALL GOOD MEN DO NOT ATTAIN
TO THE UNMEDIATED UNION WITH GOD

BUT now you may ask me why all good men do not
attain to feel this. Now listen and I will tell you the
why and the wherefore. They do not respond to
the stirring of God with a forsaking of themselves,
and so they do not abide with quickening fervour
before the Presence of God; and also they are not
careful of heart in their inward self-examination.
And therefore they always remain more outward and
manifold than inward and simple, and they work
their works more from good custom than from inward
feeling. And they care more for particular methods

and the greatness and multiplicity of good works than for the intention and love towards God. And so they remain outward and manifold of heart, and are not aware of how God lives in them with the fulness of grace.

CHAPTER VIII

SHOWING HOW THE INWARD MAN SHOULD EXERCISE HIMSELF, THAT HE MAY BE UNITED WITH GOD WITHOUT MEANS

BUT now I will tell you how the inward man, who has health amidst all miseries, should feel himself to be one with God without means. When such a quickened man rises up, with his whole being and all his powers, and joins himself to God with life-giving and active love, then he feels that his love is, in its ground, where it begins and ends, fruitive and without ground. If he then wishes to penetrate further, with his active love, into that fruitive love : then, all the powers of his soul must give way, and they must suffer and patiently endure that piercing Truth and Goodness which is God's self. For, as the air is penetrated by the brightness and heat of the sun, and iron is penetrated by fire ; so that it works through fire the works of fire, since it burns and shines like the fire ; and so likewise it can be said of the air—for, if the air had understanding, it could say : " I enlighten and brighten the whole world "—yet each of these keeps its own nature. For the fire does not become iron, and the iron does not become fire, though their union is without means; for the iron is within the fire and the fire within the iron ; and so also the air is in the sunshine and the sunshine in the air.   So likewise is God in the being of the soul ; and whenever the soul's highest powers are turned inward with active love, they are united with God without means, in a simple knowledge of all truth, and in an essential feeling and tasting of all good.   This simple knowing and feeling of God is possessed in essential love, and is practised and preserved through active love.   And therefore it is accidental to our powers through the dying introversion in love ; but it is essential to our being, and always abides within it.   And therefore we must perpetually turn inwards and be renewed in love, if we would seek out love through love.   And this is taught us by St John, where he says : HE THAT DWELLETH IN LOVE DWELLETH IN GOD AND GOD IN HIM.   And though this union of the loving spirit with God is without means, yet there is here a great distinction, for the creature never becomes God, nor does God ever become the creature ; as I explained to you heretofore in the example of the iron and the fire.   And if material things, which have been made by God, may thus be united without means ; so much the more may He, whenever such is His pleasure, unite Himself with His beloved, if they, through His grace, submit to it and make themselves ready for it.   And so in such an inward man, whom God has adorned with virtues, and, above that, has lifted up into a contemplative life, there is no intermediary between himself and God in his highest introversion but his enlightened reason and his active love.   And through these two things, he has an adherence to God ; and this is " becoming one with God," says St Bernard.   But above reason, and above active love, he is lifted up into a naked contemplation, and dwells without activity in essential love.   And there he is one love and one spirit with God, as I said heretofore.   In this essential love, through the unity which he has essentially with God, he infinitely transcends his understanding; and this is a life common to all God-seeing men.   For in this transcendence such a man is able to see in one sight— if it be God's pleasure to show it to him—all the creatures in heaven and on earth, with the distinction of their lives and their rewards.   But before the Infinity of God, he must yield, and must follow after It essentially and without end; for This no creature, not even the soul of our Lord Jesus Christ, which yet received the highest union above all other creatures, can either comprehend or overtake.

CHAPTER IX

OF THE INWARD WORKING OF GOD'S GRACE

BEHOLD, this Eternal Love, which lives within the spirit, and with which it is united without means, gives its light and its grace to all the powers of the soul; and becomes thereby the cause of all the virtues.   For the grace of God touches the highest powers of the soul, and from this touch there spring charity and the knowledge of truth, the love of all righteousness, the practice of the counsels of God according to discretion, freedom from images, the overcoming of all things without effort, and the death into the Unity through love.   As long as a man can maintain himself in this exercise, he is able to contemplate, and to feel the union without means; and he feels the touch of God within himself, which is a renewal of grace and all virtues. You must further know that the grace of God also pours forth even through the lowest powers, and touches a man's heart; and from this there comes forth a heart-felt love towards God and a sensible joy in Him; and the love and delight pierce through heart and senses, through flesh and blood, and the whole bodily nature, and cause a pressure and restlessness in all his members, so that he is often at his wit's end. For he feels like a man full of wine, who is no longer master of himself. And from this there come many a strange state, wherein men of tender heart cannot well govern themselves. Sometimes through impatient longing, they lift up their heads and gaze with wide-opened eyes towards heaven; now joying, now weeping; now singing, now crying; now in weal, now in woe, and often both together; running and jumping, laughing, clapping their hands, kneeling, bowing down: and many other like gestures are seen in them. So long as a man remains thus, and lifts himself up with an open heart towards those riches of God which live in his spirit, he feels ever anew the stirring of God, and the impatience of love; and then all these things are renewed in him. And so this man through this bodily feeling may sometimes pass into a ghostly feeling which is according to reason; and through this ghostly feeling, he may pass into a godly feeling, which is above reason; and, through this godly feeling, he may drown himself in an unchangeable and beatific feeling. This feeling is our superessential blessedness, which is a fruition of God and all His beloved: and this blessedness is that Dark Quiet which ever abides in idleness. To God it is essential, and to all creatures superessential. And there we may behold how the Persons give place and abide in the Essential Love, that is, in the Fruitive Unity; and yet they dwell for ever, according to Their personal nature, in the working of the Trinity.

CHAPTER X

OF THE MUTUAL CONTENTMENT OF THE DIVINE PERSONS, AND THE MUTUAL CONTENTMENT BETWEEN GOD AND GOOD MEN

AND so you may perceive that the Divine Nature eternally works according to the Persons, and is eternally idle and wayless according to the simplicity of Its Essence. All therefore that God has chosen and laid hold of with eternal personal love, has already been essentially and fruitively possessed of Him in unity with essential love. For the Divine Persons are enfolded within the Unity in a mutual embrace in an eternal contentment, in abysmal active love. And this is perpetually renewed in the life-giving life of the Trinity; for here there takes place a perpetual new birth in new knowledge new contentment and new outbreathing; in a new embrace, with new torrents of Eternal Love. In this content-ment all the chosen are enfolded: angels and men, from the first even to the last. Upon this content-ment depend heaven and earth, and life, and being, and the activity and preservation of all creatures, save only the tendency to turn from God in sin: this comes from the wilful and blind wickedness of the creatures. From the Divine contentment grace and glory and all gifts pour forth in heaven and on earth, and into each creature separately, according to its needs and its receptivity. For God's grace is made ready for all men, and awaits the conversion of every sinner, and whenever a sinner, urged by grace, renounces himself and will call upon God with faith, he finds pardon. And likewise, whosoever through grace with loving contentment turns towards the Eternal Contentment of God, he is enwrapped and embraced in the abysmal love which is God Himself. And thereby he is perpetually renewed in love and in the virtues; for, between our contentment in God and God's contentment in us there abides an activity of love and of eternal life. But God has eternally loved us and established us within His contentment, and if we rightly observe this, our love and our contentment shall be wakened anew. For, in the mutual relations of the Persons in the Godhead, this contentment perpetually renews itself, in a new gushing forth of love, in an ever new embrace within the Unity. And this takes place beyond Time; that is, without before and after, in an eternal NOW. For, in this embrace in the Unity, all things are consummated; and in the gushing forth of love, all things are wrought; and in the life-giving and fruitful Nature lie the power and possibilities of all things. For in the life-giving and fruitful Nature, the Son is in the Father, and the Father in the Son, and the Holy Ghost in Both. For It is a life-giving and fruitful Unity, which is the home and the beginning of all life and of all becoming. And so all creatures are therein, beyond themselves, one Being and one Life with God, as in their Eternal Origin. But in the precession of the different

Persons, the Son proceeds from the Father, and the Holy Ghost from Both : and it is there that God has made and ordained all creatures according to their proper being, and has re-made man, through His grace and His death, inasmuch as he cleaves to Him. And He has adorned His own with love and with the virtues ; and has turned back with them, towards His Origin.

There the Father and the Son and all the beloved are enfolded and embraced in the bonds of love ; that is, in the unity of the Holy Ghost. And this is that same unity which is fruitful in the outgoing activity of the Persons, and forms in Their return an eternal bond of love which shall never be untied : and all who know themselves to be bound up in it shall be blessed throughout eternity, and they are rich in virtue, and clear in contemplation, and simple in fruitive rest. For in their introversion, the Love of God is revealed to them, pouring forth with all good, and drawing back again into the Unity, and above all being and beyond all conditions abiding in eternal rest. And so they are all united with God, through means, and without means, and also without distinction.

CHAPTER XI

HOW GOOD MEN IN THEIR CONTEMPLATION HAVE THE LOVE OF GOD BEFORE THEM, AND HOW THEY ARE LIFTED UP INTO GOD

THEY have the Love of God before them in their inward seeing, as a common good pouring forth through heaven and earth ; and they feel the Holy

Trinity inclined towards them, and within them, with fulness of grace. And therefore they are adorned without and within with all the virtues, with holy practices and with good works. And thus they are united with God through Divine grace and their own holy lives. And because they have abandoned themselves to God in doing, in leaving undone, and in suffering, they have steadfast peace and inward joy, consolation and savour, of which the world cannot partake; neither any dissembler, nor the man who seeks and means himself more than the glory of God. Moreover, those same inward and enlightened men have before them in their inward seeing whenever they will, the Love of God as something drawing or urging them into the Unity; for they see and feel that the Father with the Son through the Holy Ghost, embrace Each Other and all the chosen, and draw themselves back with eternal love into the unity of Their Nature. Thus the Unity is ever drawing to itself and inviting to itself everything that has been born of It, either by nature or by grace. And therefore, too, such enlightened men are, with a free spirit, lifted up above reason into a bare and imageless vision, wherein lives the eternal indrawing summons of the Divine Unity; and, with an imageless and bare understanding, they pass through all works, and all exercises, and all things, until they reach the summit of their spirits. There, their bare understanding is drenched through by the Eternal Brightness, even as the air is drenched through by the sunshine. And the bare, uplifted will is transformed and drenched through by abysmal love, even as iron is by fire. And the bare, uplifted memory feels itself enwrapped and established in an abysmal

Absence of Image. And thereby the created image is united above reason in a threefold way with its Eternal Image, which is the origin of its being and its life ; and this origin is preserved and possessed, essentially and eternally, through a simple seeing in an imageless void : and so a man is lifted up above reason in a threefold manner into the Unity, and in a onefold manner into the Trinity. Yet the creature does not become God, for the union takes place in God through grace and our homeward-turning love : and therefore the creature in its inward contemplation feels a distinction and an otherness between itself and God. And though the union is without means, yet the manifold works which God works in heaven and on earth are nevertheless hidden from the spirit. For though God gives Himself as He is, with clear discernment, He gives Himself in the essence of the soul, where the powers of the soul are simplified above reason, and where, in simplicity, they suffer the transformation of God.   There all is full and overflowing, for the spirit feels itself to be one truth and one richness and one unity with God. Yet even here there is an essential tending forward, and therein is an essential distinction between the being of the soul and the Being of God ; and this is the highest and finest distinction which we are able to feel.

CHAPTER XII

OF THE HIGHEST UNION, WITHOUT DIFFERENCE OR DISTINCTION

AND after this there follows the union without distinction. For you must apprehend the Love of God not only as an outpouring with all good, and as drawing back again into the Unity ; but it is also, above all distinction, an essential fruition in the bare Essence of the Godhead. And in consequence of this enlightened men have found within themselves an essential contemplation which is above reason and without reason, and a fruitive tendency which pierces through every condition and all being, and through which they immerse themselves in a wayless abyss of fathomless beatitude, where the Trinity of the Divine Persons possess Their Nature in the essential Unity. Behold, this beatitude is so onefold and so wayless that in it every essential gazing, tendency, and creaturely distinction cease and pass away. For by this fruition, all uplifted spirits are melted and noughted in the Essence of God, Which is the super-essence of all essence. There they fall from themselves into a solitude and an ignorance which are fathomless ; there all light is turned to darkness ; there the three Persons give place to the Essential Unity, and abide without distinction in fruition of essential blessedness. This blessedness is essential to God, and superessential to all creatures ; for no created essence can become one with God's Essence and pass away from its own substance. For so the creature would become God, which is impossible ; for the Divine Essence can neither wax nor wane, nor can anything be added to It or taken from It. Yet all loving spirits are one fruition and one blessedness with God without distinction ; for that beatific state, which is the fruition of God and of all His beloved, is so simple and onefold that therein neither Father, nor Son, nor Holy Ghost, is distinct according to the Persons, neither is any creature. But all en-

lightened spirits are here lifted up above themselves
into a wayless fruition, which is an abundance beyond
all the fulness that any creature has ever received
or shall ever receive. For there all uplifted spirits
are, in their superessence, one fruition and one
beatitude with God without distinction ; and there
this beatitude is so onefold that no distinction can
enter into it. And this was prayed for by Christ
when He besought His Father in heaven that all His
beloved might be made perfect in one, even as He is
one with the Father through the Holy Ghost : even
so He prayed and besought that He in us and we in
Him and His heavenly Father might be one in fruition
through the Holy Ghost. And this I think the most
loving prayer which Christ ever made for our
blessedness.

CHAPTER XIII

OF THE THREEFOLD PRAYER OF CHRIST, THAT WE MIGHT BE ONE WITH GOD

BUT you should also observe that His prayer, as it
has been written by St John in this same Gospel, was
threefold. For He prayed that we might be with
Him, that we might behold the glory which His
Father had given Him. And therefore I said at the
beginning that all good men are united with God by
means of Divine grace and their own virtuous life ;
for the love of God is always pouring into us with new
gifts, and whosoever is aware of this is fulfilled with
new virtues and holy exercises and with all good, in
the way that I told you heretofore : and this union
through the fulness of grace and glory, in body and

soul, begins here below and shall endure throughout
eternity.

Further, Christ prayed thus, that He might be in us
and we in Him.   This we find in the Gospel, in many
places.   And this is the union without means ; for the
Love of God is not only outpouring, but it also draws
us inwards, into the Unity.   And those who feel and
are aware of this, become inward and enlightened
men, and their highest powers are uplifted, above all
exercises, into their naked being : and there, above
reason, the powers become simplified in their essence,
and so they are full and overflowing.   For in that
simplicity, the spirit finds itself united with God
without means ; and this union, with the exercise
which belongs to it, shall endure eternally, as I have
told you heretofore.

Further, Christ uttered His most sublime prayer,
namely, that His beloved might be made perfect in
one, as He is one with the Father : not one as He is
with the Father one single Divine Substance, for this
is impossible to us ; but so one, and in such a unity,
as He is one fruition and one beatitude with the
Father without distinction in Essential Love.   Those
who are thus united with God in this threefold way,
in them the prayer of Christ has been fulfilled.

> These with God shall ebb and flow,
> Having and joying, they shall empty go ;
> They shall both work and passively endure,
> And in their superessence rest secure.
> They shall go out and in, and find their food,
> And, drunk with love, in radiant darkness sleep in God.

Many more words I should like to say here, but
those who possess this have no need of them : and

he to whom it has been shown, and who cleaves with love to Love, he shall be taught the whole truth by Love itself. But those who turn outwards, and would find consolation in outward things, do not feel this ; and, even though I should say much more of it, yet they would not understand. For those who give themselves wholly to outward works, or those who are idle in inward passivity, shall never be able to understand it. Now although reason and all bodily feelings must here give place and yield to the faith and contemplation of the spirit,　　and to those things which are above reason ; yet reason and also the life of the senses continue to abide in their place, and cannot pass away, any more than the nature of man can pass away. And further, though the gazing and tendency of the spirit towards God must give place to fruition in simplicity ; yet this gazing and this tendency continue to exist in their place.　　For this is the inmost life of the spirit ; and, in the enlightened and uplifted man, the life of the senses adheres to the spirit. And so his sensual powers are joined to God by heart-felt love, and his nature is fulfilled with all good ; and he feels that his ghostly life adheres to God without means. And thereby his highest powers are uplifted to God in eternal love, and drenched through by Divine truth, and established in imageless freedom. And so he is filled with God, and overflowing without measure. In this inundation there comes to pass the essential outpouring or immersion in the superessential Unity ; and this is the union without distinction, of which I have often told you. For in the superessence all our ways end. If we will go with God upon the highway of love, we shall rest with Him

eternally and without end : and thus we shall eternally go forth towards God and enter into Him and
rest in Him.

CHAPTER XIV

HERE THE AUTHOR DECLARES THAT HE SUBMITS ALL
THAT HE HAS WRITTEN TO THE JUDGMENT OF HOLY
CHURCH

Now at this time I cannot set forth my meaning more
clearly. In all that I understand, or feel, or have
written, I submit myself to the judgment of the saints
and of Holy Church ; for I wish to live and to die
as a servant of Christ, in the Christian faith ; and I
desire to be, by the grace of God, a life-giving member
of Holy Church. And therefore, as I told you heretofore, you should beware of those self-deceived men
who, by means of their idle vacancy, and with their
bare and simple gaze have found the Divine Essence
within themselves in a merely natural way ; and
who pretend to be one with God without the grace
of God, and without exercise of virtue, and without
obedience to God and to Holy Church. And for all
their perversity of life, which I have described, they
would be one with God's Son by nature. But if the
Prince of all the angels was cast out of heaven, because
he set himself up against God and would be like unto
the most High ; and if the first man was driven from
Paradise because he would be as God : how then shall
this wretched sinner—that is, the faithless Christian
who would be as God without likeness to God in
grace and virtue—ever rise from earth into heaven ?
For through his own power no man has ascended

into heaven, save the Son of Man, Jesus Christ. And therefore we must unite ourselves with Him, through grace and virtue and Christian faith : so we shall ascend with Him whither He has gone before us. For in the Last Day we shall all rise, each with his own body ; and then those who have worked good works shall go into life everlasting, and those who have worked evil works shall go into everlasting fire. These are two unlike ends, which shall never come together ; for each flies from the other perpetually.

Pray for him who has composed and written this, that God may have mercy upon him. That his poor beginning, and his and our wretched middle course, may be brought to a blessed end, this may Jesus Christ, the Son of the living God, bestow upon us all. AMEN.